IS IT JUST ME OR HAS THE SHIT HIT THE FAN?

STEVE LOWE AND ALAN McARTHUR

D0312136

sphere

SPHERE

First published in Great Britain in 2009 by Sphere

A CIP catalogue record for this book
is available from the British Library.

ISBN 978-1-84744-365-6

Typeset in Palatino by M Rules
Printed and bound in Great Britain by
Clays Ltd, St Ives plc

Papers used by Sphere are natural, renewable and recyclable
products sourced from well-managed forests and certified
in accordance with the rules of the Forest Stewardship Council.

 Mixed Sources
Product group from well-managed
forests and other controlled sources
www.fsc.org Cert no. SGS-COC-004081
© 1996 Forest Stewardship Council

FSC

Sphere
An imprint of
Little, Brown Book Group
100 Victoria Embankment
London EC4Y 0DY

An Hachette UK Company
www.hachette.co.uk

www.littlebrown.co.uk

IS IT JUST ME OR HAS THE SHIT HIT THE FAN?

YOUR HILARIOUS NEW GUIDE TO
UNREMITTING GLOBAL MISERY

A

Aldi, Middle classes discovering

Shopping at Aldi – it's the new thing! Not because it's cheap or anything, but because it's cool. The Sunday supplements are all raving about the rise of the Aldirati. When a new discount supermarket opens, there are queues around the block like they're handing out free Croatian villas rather than just cheap deli items, power tools and Azerbaijani pork scratchings.

Of course, despite all the broadsheet ravings, these shops actually existed before the recession. Selling much the same stuff. But the chattering classes have to discover these things as they might an entirely new continent . . .

'Dolmades. So many dolmades. For a quid. And they're from Germany. German dolmades, the finest dolmades in all the world. Well, they're not, but they're a quid. And all the cold meats: bresaola, Parma ham . . . it's one big cold meat platter round our house now. I've even started handing it out in the street. They say I'm cold meat crazy!

'Then there's the biscuits covered in luminous sweets, "Disco Biscuits". Don't worry though, *these* Disco Biscuits are perfectly legal. Although sometimes I think they shouldn't be!

'And the welder's safety set. At £9.99, I couldn't refuse.

You should see our garage – it's like a shipyard out there.

'Jane got a complete set of machine-cast monkey wrenches. From Libya or something. A pound! Heaven knows what she thinks she's going to do with them. Tinker with the combine harvester we got in Lidl I expect. Do you know Lidl? It's like Netto only a smidge more *us* . . .'

A-list tot rivals

There's a new kid in town. Kids.

'The little ballerina: Suri Cruise skips out of dance class in battered pink pumps . . . She's certainly become a style icon for a generation of pre-schoolers.'

Now that's a fucked-up sentence. Even by *Daily Mail* standards that's a fucked-up sentence.

But, oh, hang on . . . 'Suri Cruise now has a rival for the title of Hollywood's most adorable toddler.' (What? You're shitting me?) 'Shiloh, the daughter of Brad Pitt and Angelina Jolie, proved herself a worthy contender during a family outing in Washington DC over the weekend.'

But I thought Suri was, like, the hottest kid?

Ah, don't worry, though, because the *Sun* says: 'Tom Cruise and Katie Holmes' daughter Suri (with her thick dark hair and wide eyes . . .) has been named the most "influential" A-list toddler in a new *Forbes* list. The two-year-old beat Brad Pitt and Angelina Jolie's kids . . .'

Forbes has an Influential Toddler list. *Forbes* has an Influential Toddler list. *Forbes* has, it bears repeating, an Influential Toddler list.

But: 'Watch out Suri! Little Shiloh Jolie-Pitt could take the A-list tot's cutie crown . . . the cherubic two-year-old . . . has inherited her father's piercing blue eyes and her mother's famous pout . . . She also brought along her favourite security blanket and a cuddly toy for the afternoon.'

Yes, she'll be needing that security blanket with all these freaks on her case. And to think these papers are usually quite down on paedophilia.

All-Nations credit crunch blame game, The

Well, the French and Germans are pretty clear on who to blame: Britain and America, the Anglo-Saxon baddies. Actually, given the years of hearing Gordon Brown boasting about how Europe should follow Britain's deregulated lead, it's surprising they don't shout: 'Ah ha! You tit!' But then that wouldn't be diplomatic.

Brazilian President Lula da Silva went further, blaming 'the irrational behaviour of white people with blue eyes'. For a moment I thought he was talking about me . . . White? Blue eyes? Irrational behaviour? Then I remembered I wasn't even there.

The British responded to these taunts gallantly. That is, they blamed the Americans. This is alarming. You can't have Anglo-Saxons falling out with each other. What kind of defence will they be able to mount when the Vikings come? Did anyone in the government think about that? One word, people: Lindisfarne. Are you okay with that?

So who did America blame? Well, Treasury Secretary Timothy Geithner said the Chinese were keeping the yen low to create a trade imbalance . . . and that the Beijing Olympics was 'rubbish'.

And who did the Chinese blame? The Americans. Boring! They should have said the Turks and Caicos Islands, that would have got people thinking.

But there was another old peril lurking too. One that was almost too noxious to name. This could be gleaned from the *Telegraph* story headlined: 'Germany's slump risks explosive mood'. The nudging implication being you know what happens when Germany gets in an explosive mood.

Actually, they found the peril could be named. The text was accompanied by a picture of the Reichstag, captioned: 'The country's politicians will hope any slump does not lead to the sort of civil unrest which saw this building catch fire in 1933.'

Maybe we can't pin this one on Germany, but haven't they been responsible for enough? We're just saying . . . blue eyes, white skin, *blond hair*? The War, people. *The ruddy War!*

Anyway, weren't the Saxons originally from Germany? So who looks stupid now, eh?

And the Angles actually came from Denmark, so let's not forget those bastards either.

With their so-called chairs.

Peter Andre's *Insania* actually being highly prescient

Look him in the eyes and tell him he was wrong.

Ann Summers' Mother's Day window promotions

As in big window stickers reminding you that Mother's Day is imminent. Like at Clinton Cards, but in the window of a shop selling sex toys, lacy basques and lubricants of an intimate nature. This promotion was real and I know because I saw it.

Am I a prude for thinking this is wrong? Where would you start if, say, the assistant asked you what kind of things your mum usually likes? And choosing the right gift is a minefield anyway. What's the returns policy here? 'You know, if she doesn't get off on PVC after all? In the packaging, obviously – I mean, I'm not going to bring it back after she's done vigorous sex in it or anything . . .'

And you definitely wouldn't want to be involved in a conversation anything like this one:

CHRIS: Hey Mum! Happy Mother's Day! I got you a Rabbit.

MUM: Oh, I'm not sure about pets at my age. Where would I keep it?

CHRIS: Erm . . .

Arctic melting news reports saying that previous reports about the Arctic melting understated the problem

Every time I see a report about the Arctic melting, it says that previous reports about the Arctic melting understated the problem. So common sense tells me that this new report – the one disrespecting all the previous reports about the Arctic melting – will probably turn out to be an under-statement too.

And you know the report about the Arctic melting that comes after that? Yeah, well I reckon that will turn out to be an underestimate. Unless people start actually doing some-thing about stopping the Arctic melting, which would be cool, then the Arctic might just carry on doing what it's doing: melting.

I'm not looking for a Nobel prize here. I'm just calling it like I see it. And I see all sorts, and I say this: surprise has had its day. Surprise is over. Don't bother being surprised *any more*.

Because nature is up to something. Not just the melting, all of it. These are just some of the recent events I've been able to tune into by reading tabloid newspapers on the toilet:

1. The swan that mated with a pedalo
2. The monkey in a German zoo that stored up rocks to throw at visitors
3. The seal that raped a penguin
4. The cow that attacked David Blunkett
5. The sea lion in *another* German zoo that literally fucked until it died (he was called Mike)
6. The man in Dorset who rides a zebra to the pub
7. The general rise in attacks on people by cows

Shit like this is going to start happening with increasing regularity.

On a more hopeful note, I did read about a dog that nur-tured an owl. The spaniel took to the owl at its owners' bird of prey centre in Cornwall, and started licking it clean now and again. Even after it was released into the wild, the owl returned several times a day to get licked clean by his four-legged friend and generally to hang out. 'It's a friendship that will never die,' said the owner.

Hold on to that. It's beautiful.

Auschwitz being mistaken for a brand of beer

I'm all for dumbing down, but this is poor. To mark the DVD release of the children's' Holocaust movie *The Boy in the Striped Pyjamas*, a survey found a quarter of eleven-to-sixteen-year-olds in the UK had no idea what Auschwitz was. Or, if they did have an idea, it was a *really* weird idea. Some thought it was a religious festival, others a country next to Germany. And then there were the ones who thought it was a brand of beer. Sorry, but that's just a bit thick, isn't it? A beer?!? So what are the gas chambers – where they put the bubbles in?

B

Bags for life that aren't

'Bags for life! Bags for life! We're going to save the world with our bags for life!'

That's the start of the 'Bags For Life' song. It's pretty jaunty. I wrote it myself, so overtaken was I by the liberating possibilities of the bag for life.

Hang on, though. This bag for life is in bits – and I'm still alive! Maybe they're not going to save the world after all. Maybe that's too much for any bag. Maybe we're fucked after all, even after we bought, like, a bag.

Aaaaarrrghhhhhhhh!

Ed Balls

Ed Balls is very much synonymous with Gordon Brown. Balls' wife, Yvette Cooper, is also a confirmed Brownite. The Balls are in Gordon's court. Indeed, some would say that Brown's closest political allies are his Balls. If his Balls were in trouble, Brown would help. There is no way Brown would hang his Balls out to dry.

When Balls was caught 'flipping' – changing the house that he and Cooper designated as their 'second home' for

MP's expenses purposes – three times in a two-year period, Brown protected his Balls and didn't let his Balls dangle free. Brown likes a safe home for his Balls. Or two safe homes.

Indeed, shortly afterwards, Brown tried to make his Balls Chancellor of the Exchequer. Brown hoped to berth his Balls next door, where he could get easy access to them.

But his Balls are divisive. Some regard Brown's Balls with deep suspicion, briefing that if Brown insisted on forcing his Balls forward at such a time, the situation could prove 'explosive'.

He could have forced the issue, but Alistair Darling – who was 'distressed' as he had once been very close to Brown's Balls – said he would not make way for Brown's Balls, and he didn't have the balls to put his Balls on top of his Darling, and promote his Balls by handing his Darling the sack.

So instead his Balls had to stay in charge of the schools. Even so, don't ever make the mistake of thinking you have heard the last of Brown's Balls.

For Brown's Balls will rise again.

Bank bailouts

The potential collapse of capitalism is definitely something worth recording *Newsnight* for. Here are just some of the things that have stuck in my mind about the banking collapse:

1. At the time of the UK bank bailout in October 2008, the banks were twenty-four hours away

from total implosion. The word 'bankrupt' comes from the Middle Latin *banca rupta* meaning 'bank broken', which is what the banks were. Failed, derelict, bust, *kaput*, useless, shit, failed, washed-up, broken, bollocks . . . these are just some of the words you can use to describe how fucked they were. And government money was the only option. Cash-rich Asia and Saudi Arabia would not lend ('Leave us alone, skint guys'). No one would lend, not even Ocean Finance. But the bankers did not like their new 'over a barrel' status. At frantic Treasury meetings, they were appalled at the lack of food laid on and at being forced to scuttle across Parliament Street to buy sandwiches at Tesco Metro. These people should not be expected to buy their own sandwiches! They have spent the past decade cultivating the lifestyles of rock stars who are also military dictators. They should be *showered* in sandwiches. Literally *showered* in Tesco packet sandwiches.

2. They really did almost bring down the world financial system. The collapse of insurer AIG was 'close to an extinction-level event', said the *New York Times*. Even George W. couldn't fail to see that 'this sucker could go down', as, in the fine words of one fund manager, 'banks fell over like fat Labradors running over a wet kitchen floor'. Which makes it sound like more of a laugh than it really was.

3. The swashbuckling, go-getting, live-by-the-

market-die-by-the-market guys found they did like some safety nets after all. Not ones for the poor, perhaps, but definitely ones for the rich. How much were we lending them? In July 2009, the IMF revealed the UK taxpayer bailout was £904 billion. Or, to put it another way, £904,000,000,000. Or, to put it another way, roughly £15,000 for every member of the population. Or, to put it another way, nine-hundred-and-four billion pounds. Or, to put it another way, FUCKING FUCKING FUCK!!

4. Don't worry, though. Because we'll get it back, maybe, at some point, if the banking system keeps its head and the economy recovers (hardly racing certainties). On Will Hutton's calculations, we might only lose something like £100 billion for ever. Anyway, it's only money. Didn't Adam Smith say that money isn't real but just 'a matter of belief'? But it's *our* matter of belief. The matter of belief we'd been saving up (quite literally) for our retirement.

5. This 'much emulated' giving-of-money-to-banks was billed as a brave and bold decision. But where was the bravery, really? The banks weren't exactly in a great position, being skint. Imagine the reforms you could push through. Tax reforms! Green reforms! Radical reforms! In the event, Brown bravely extracted . . . sweet shite all. He was cross with them, I'll give him that. As he gave them the money, he wasn't smiling (and thank Christ for that). All they had

to do was lend this money to help stimulate the economy. And did they manage that? Not really, no. Then again, why would they? They had loads of toxic debt to make up for. And the government *didn't even say they had to.*

6. Still, Brown couldn't get too shirty, having trumpeted 'limited touch' regulation of the bankers more than anyone (limited touch regulation being like light touch regulation, only lighter). In a Mansion House speech in June 2007, a few days before he swapped Number 11 for Number 10, he said: 'This is an era that history will record as a golden age for the City of London. I want to thank you . . .' Brown went on to praise the City's 'creativity and ingenuity' in creating 'the most modern instruments of finance'. He also pointed out that, post-Enron and WorldCom scandals, 'many who advised me . . . favoured a regulatory crackdown. I believe we were right not to go down that road.' Arsehole.

7. Revealing where the banking elites' hearts lay in all this . . . as the US government unveiled its TARP bailout plan (buying up the toxic debt at above-market rates), the bankers had one, and only one, caveat, on which they were obsessively insistent. Don't limit our pay and bonuses. This was their *only* demand. Anything else: making us stand on chairs, making us speak French, dictating the jaunty angle at which we should wear our hats, fine – just please, don't take away our

bonuses! Not very sophisticated people, you would have to say. The US government replied: 'Cool.'

8. The lights came on and the neoliberal nonsense was proved, once and for all, to be a heap of mad shit. Even former Chairman of the Federal Reserve Alan Greenspan – the daddy of no-regulations capitalism, hero to Brown, disciple of crazy right-wing/sado-masochist novelist Ayn Rand – had to go before Congress and say: 'Er, you know what, I might have been a bit wrong.' No fucking shit, Sherlock Shitsticks! Not that we need to do too much rethinking here. Even Obama, who is *all about change,* doesn't want that much change. In July 2009, Alistair Darling published a white paper on cleaning up banking – the first ten pages being praise for the City (well, they have had it tough lately). One financial expert said Darling had 'plumped for fudge'. Which is fair enough, maybe he likes fudge. Then the Treasury Select Committee called the proposed reforms 'largely cosmetic'. Well, maybe he likes cosmetics too. Look, let's just ease that train back on the rails. Careful now. Nearly there. Yes, that's better. Okay, so the rails are still heading towards that great big cliff. But let's worry about that later. (Like, say, when we have fallen off the cliff.)

9. Bonuses are back! This is the slogan ringing round Wall Street and the City in 2009. Goldman Sachs' 2009 bonuses actually topped those of

2007. So it's back to 'normal' then, even though 'normal' also means 'mental'. Every minor building society that ever held a bean throwing it round made-up markets in the hope the party will never end. Countries competing to be the helipad of global capital, to be 'the world's biggest tax haven' (the IMF's assessment of the UK), home to the most Russian oligarchs, and the guys privatising the South American water supplies (you know, all the cool guys) . . . Our very civilisation relies on us getting the system working again, so traders can put their days to good use hyping commodity bubbles, turning a quick buck pushing up food prices (one pesky side-effect being more people starving). Pension funds do well out of it, though, so why would anyone *want* to change? And what have these people got to lose? If we bailed them out once, we'll do it again. Yes, they've been bad, but what's a world without a little bad? Too fast to live, too big to fail. Bonuses are back!

10. The cunts didn't even say thank you. THIS IS NO WAY TO RUN A FUCKING WORLD.

Heston Blumenthal always having to be different

Celebrity chefs, almost to a man/woman, reacted to the recession in exactly the same way. By experiencing massive money problems.

But where other celebrity chefs fell into dire financial difficulties, Heston Blumenthal took a different tack: he closed his restaurant after his customers started throwing up everywhere. He always does like to stand out from the crowd.

His Fat Duck, in Berkshire, once named the Best Restaurant in the World, had to shut after customers started chucking their guts up. It was the best vomit in the world, some of them said. Weirdly, shortly after reopening it was named the second-best restaurant in the world.

Shouldn't the second-best restaurant in the world ideally be one that has not just been forced to close because everyone is throwing up everywhere? Fucking hell, what's the third best like?

In the struggle to be different, nothing is off limits. Blumenthal told one newspaper: 'I'm not the world's most romantic man. For Valentine's my daughter gave me a cup of tea and a bunch of roses in bed. At the time I was working on a recipe and I was frustrated I couldn't find strong enough rose-flavoured roses. I didn't even think about it; I tore off the petals, put them in my mouth and started munching them.'

You probably get used to that kind of thing being Heston Blumenthal's daughter.

'Have you seen my mobile anywhere?'

'I think Dad ate it . . .'

'Try ringing it.'

'Yeah, Dad ate it.'

BNP bloggers

BNP bloggers are 'oddballs', 'Walter Mitty characters', 'compulsive liars' who 'get carried away with conspiracy theories'. 'Born troublemakers', they 'can't write proper English'.

So says, er, the BNP, in an internal training manual for party organisers. And for once I agree with them.

The manual urges apparatchiks to stop members setting up BNP-related websites, lest the public cotton on to what fuckwits they are.

But really, how likely is that?

BNP coppers

When the BNP's membership list was leaked in November 2008, many people expressed surprise that there were police officers on it.

To which you have to ask: have you actually met any coppers?

Or seen that documentary about the Hendon police training college rife with racists – the one where they dressed up like the Klan?

Or heard about the entrenched 'canteen culture'? (A strange phrase, implying all canteens are hotbeds of racist barracking: 'Would you like anything to drink with that, love? Or was it just the racist barracking you were after? Cutlery's over there, can you wipe down your tray after?')

Or remember the Essex WPC sacked for having a mannequin dressed up like an SS officer in her house?

Or actually met any coppers?

The Association of Chief Police Officers, which has banned police officers and staff from belonging to the BNP, called on forces to investigate.

So while the BNP were demanding the police investigate the leaking of the list, the police were demanding that the police investigate the police *on* the list. Which they did.

The best thing about the list – and no other political parties do this, surely? – is that it listed members' hobbies, which included things like steam railways, paganism and line-dancing. It's good to know white supremacy leaves time for other, fun activities and that they're not just obsessed by race war. They also like line-dancing. Whatever did happen to Billy Ray Cyrus? That's what the British Nazis want to know.

There was also the driving instructor who offered discounts for BNP members. And, of course, the antiques dealer who owned two fourteenth- and fifteenth-century suits of armour, who could 'joust for rallies'. With attractions like that, no wonder the mainstream parties are struggling to compete.

And I almost felt sorry for the lapsed member who 'Objects to being told he shouldn't wear a bomber jacket'. That's a bit much. Whipping up door-to-door ethnic hate: fine. Wearing a bomber jacket: no, sorry, that's just the kind of outmoded behaviour we're trying to move beyond. You can keep that sort of thing at home, you fascist.

BNP jamborees

If BNP summer camps didn't sound fun enough on their own – and by God, they do, don't they? – 'Junior Patriots' can indulge themselves with the BNP's new comic, *The Comet*, featuring crazy cartoon character Billy Brit and his hilarious racist antics.

They can log on to the website to enjoy a puppet of Billy reciting 'educational poems'. In one, 'Heroes', Billy educates us about great British racists past:

> He gave a speech called Rivers Of Blood and never
>   gave up the fight.
> Enoch Powell spoke for me.
> And Enoch Powell was white.

And what kid these days doesn't like really shit racist puppets? You know, shit puppets reciting poems about Enoch Powell?

Junior Patriots also get ID cards, a newsletter and a training book with lessons in 'ethno nationalism'. They are invited to the BNP's annual youth camp and two further training camps where they learn 'shooting', 'self defence', 'flag drills' and 'nationalist ideology'. Ah, those long hot summers of 'nationalist ideology'. Those long hot summers of 'nationalist ideology' under the care of a bull-necked psycho with convictions for racially motivated violence.

Maybe it's like church school, where you don't really have to believe in it all – you can just appreciate the discipline. Wonder what their OFSTED report's like.

Bono: corporate-raiding tax dodger

Bono is changing his name from Bono Vox, meaning 'good voice', to Bono 'Corporate-Raiding Tax Dodger' Vox. He just likes the way it sounds.

U2 moved their publishing arm to Holland, a tax haven, despite Ireland itself being something of a tax haven. It's famous for it. In Ireland, they would have paid 12.5 per cent tax on royalty payments compared to Holland's 5 per cent. 12.5 per cent? It's hardly squeezing till the pips squeak, is it? And Ireland could do with the money at the moment. It's famous for it.

When U2 made this move, some accused corporate-raiding tax dodger Bono of hypocrisy and, in a way, if you look at it closely, you can see where these people are coming from . . . he's the little donate-more-tax-money-to-Africa feller. Trade! Aid! That's him. So, he's all for the donating tax money to Africa, despite himself being a dodger of taxes – the taxes you need some of if you are going to donate taxes to Africa. Unless he's not actually in U2? No, he is. He's the singer.

And of the tax-dodging band U2, it's only corporate-raiding tax dodger Bono who decided to become a corporate raider, investing some of his vast wealth in the private equity fund Elevation Partners. (Yes, the company is named after the U2 song, 'Elevation'. Do they play the song at meetings? Perhaps punching the air shouting 'E-Le-Va-Tion'? Don't know for sure, but . . . yeah, they do.)

What was it that attracted him to the controversial world of private equity investment? Well, it could be the sector's reputation for ripping companies to pieces –

which does sound pretty rock'n'roll and has earned them the nickname of 'locusts' (and we know he's already got the shades for that). Or maybe he just got excited about the associations of 'stripping' in 'asset stripping' – I know I do.

Or maybe it's just the potential for massive profit, what with private equity being a neat system for wealthy investors to borrow shitloads more money to buy up companies for 'restructuring' – sacking people, selling properties – before selling them on, so becoming the latest incarnation of wealth creaming off more wealth for the already highly wealthy – the centuries-old trick that has left whole continents beggared, including the one Bono likes. Holland. No, Africa, I meant Africa.

Reportedly a minor laughing stock, Elevation did make a mini-splash by buying a stake in pro-inequality bible *Forbes*, the magazine that celebrates the bastard billionaires who fucked the world (they usually word it differently) – even doing puff pieces on Allen Stanford as the fraud investigations piled up around his chubby neck. I'm not saying Bono actually wrote the articles himself or anything. Equally, I'm not saying he didn't. I don't actually know.

Anyway, when asked how all this squared with Bono's humanitarian mission, Elevation co-founder Roger McNamee explained: 'The way you solve poverty is giving people the tools to overcome it.' So that's raising up the world's poor by being a corporate-raiding tax dodger, then. In an ideal world, we'd all be doing it. At the moment, that's just a dream but maybe, one day, we will be able to live in a world where anyone who wants to can be a corporate - raiding tax dodger.

Of course, it's been calculated that tax-avoidance-driven capital flight costs developing countries ten times what they receive in aid. So Bono's example is giving tools to *someone*, anyway. Go, tiny cowboy, go!

Brit *auteur* feelgood flicks

Mike Leigh's *Happy-Go-Lucky* and Ken Loach's *Looking for Eric* render them both as nothing more (or less) than turncoats. We were warned to expect feelgood escapist films in response to the recession – Jennifer Aniston, puppies, Abba, all that. But not from this pair.

We expected better – or rather, worse. Timothy Spall breaking down again, some truly awful Scottish estates, Cathy not coming home, Cathy *never* coming home. But no: it's all happy-go-lucky (happy!) young women gadding about in London and 'ooh, ah Cantona'.

These are times of austerity, of unemployment, of conflict, these are *your times*! And what do you give us? Irrepressible cheeriness and football-related whimsy? Hell's fucking happy teeth! Why not bring on the showgirls and be done? Get Pixar in, why don't you? Animate the fuckers.

Although, having said this, *Ooh, Ah Cantona* is still recognisably a Ken Loach film in that it does feature as its central character a very depressed postman.

Broadsheet darlings for ten minutes

Ooh look, it's Beth Ditto. It's Beth Ditto. It's Beth Ditto. It's Beth Ditto. It's Beth Ditto. It's Beth Ditto. It's Beth Ditto. Ooh. Beth Ditto. Ditto. It's Beth Ditto. Etc.

Brown bag couture

The trouble with the new era is that it can leave people feeling left out. Like there's no place for them in today's world.

We're talking about the loaded. People who, through no fault of their own, were loaded before, are loaded now, and will still be loaded when whatever happens next happens next. People are suffering out there. This can be alienating – especially for those who are not suffering.

Milton Pedraza of New York consultants the Luxury Institute (what names!) explained why conspicuous consumption was O-U-T. 'Some of them realise it can appear offensive to people, and they don't want to be the poster child for greed or insensitivity.'

They do want to be greedy and insensitive, but not appear on the posters.

But there is still a way to join in – or at least disguise the fact that you're not joining in – get your couture purchases delivered to the office in brown paper bags. Rubbing other people's noses in it is so yesterday. Now there's 'brown bag couture'. Stealth wealth!

Forbes magazine's list of 'Ten Ways To Buy Luxury, Discreetly' revealed tips for the stealthily wealthy: basically, just buy expensive stuff that isn't covered in Gucci or Chanel logos. Obvious, really.

Oh, and this little nugget: 'Another example of understated luxury is Denyse Schmidt's patchwork quilt designs. The quilts are special because they're hand-quilted by Amish craftswomen with pre-washed, fine cotton fabrics . . . Sure, they cost upward of $6,000, but only you will know the uniqueness of the blanket draping your rocking chair.'

In ways such as this, you *can* rub other people's noses in it, but without them even knowing! It'll just be your little secret. Your rubby-nosey secret. It's almost kinky, actually.

Carla Bruni picture auctions

Pictures of Carla Bruni in the nude. This is what gets auctioned these days.

I like to think the great auction houses of the world – Bonham's, Christie's – are right now devoting entire wings to these items: 'And over here there's another fine example, probably dating from . . . oh, I would say, the mid-1990s. Look, you can see her tits. But not her muff. Not properly.'

Amazing, the whole Carla Bruni thing. On one level, if she wants to sex up Sarkozy's presidency, whatever. But it gets to weird levels when a much-syndicated photo of the couple emerging from voting in the Euro elections has her pouting into the camera with erect nipples perkily poking through her white blouse. I mean, how do you even do that? Voting in the Euro elections? Was it just really cold or something? But it was June!

Absolutely senseless.

Businesses that didn't pass on the VAT cut

It might only be two-and-a-half-pence – but it's MY two-and-a-half-pence, you chiselling fucknuts.

C

Vince Cable

Liberal Democrat Treasury Spokesman Vince Cable has 'had a good recession'. People love him. Good old Vince. 'He is a golden interlude in Lib Dem history,' said Simon Carr in the *Independent*. 'He is a holiday in Tuscany.' (The Tuscany thing doesn't make ANY SENSE, but you can see where people are going with this.)

Some even say Vince Cable would make a better Lib Dem leader than the current incumbent. Although to make that judgement with any authority, they'd have to be able to remember who the current incumbent is.

So what does Cable's appeal amount to? Basically, him popping up on the telly all the time saying he doesn't think it's a good idea – and never has thought it a good idea – for deluded young men on drugs to throw borrowed money around semi-made-up international junk markets like it's fucking water.

It's hard to disagree with this assertion.

He also doesn't think – and he's been consistent here too – that houses should cost so much money that no one can actually afford them.

It's also hard to disagree with this assertion. (Although, you know, I *could* – if I wanted to.)

It helps that Cable looks sensible. He doesn't look like he's going to get fucked up on drugs and throw borrowed money about like water anytime soon. Not old Vince.

So he's dependable. But what does he actually want to *do*? Er, not much.

He is, after all, a Liberal Democrat. The party that faces right or left depending on the audience and that tends to privatise things with gusto if it ever get its mitts on a local council. The party with an economic policy that basically amounts to: do more or less what you're doing now, but for God's sake do it *sensibly*. The environment? Well, let's be sensible about it.

So, for Cable – a member of the 'fairer taxes, not higher taxes', free marketeer, amenable-to-a-coalition-with-the-Tories centre-right wing of the Lib Dems – it's 'Fucking watch out! It's a storm! An apocalypse! But don't meddle too much – don't meddle too much, in this apocalypse.'

So balls to Vince Cable, basically. You can fucking keep him.

Anyway, he's not even that sensible. One of the weirder titbits to come out in the MPs' expenses scandal was that BT and British Gas were always threatening to cut off his office phone because the bill hadn't been paid.

You want to get a direct debit, mate. Even I know that.

Casino councils

Of all the people caught with their high-risk banking trousers down, it really shouldn't have been councils.

At the time of the Icelandic bank collapse, UK councils had almost a billion pounds invested there. That's a lot of Meals on Wheels, that is. Approximately three-quarters of a billion meals on a quarter of a million wheels – i.e. fifty thousand vans, allowing for one spare wheel each – in fact.

'So that's the apologies. Now I believe we're going to have a finance report from Councillor Barraclough.'

'Yes, indeed, thank you. Well, as of the last meeting I am happy to report that we have basically spunked everything on the buccaneering high seas of hyper-leverage silly-money offshore banking. We just thought, You know what? Fuck it! The interest rates were unbelievable. Also, we realised we had always wanted to be buccaneers but never had the opportunity before. It can be quite boring being us, writing the odd cheque and stuff, so we thought we'd sex it up a bit.

'Yes, we were warned several times that we were being silly arses. And, yes, we were going to get all the money back and put it in the Post Office. But you know how it is with boring shit like that. You just never seem to get round to it.

'So, in essence, to sum up, as I believe the phrase has it . . . mum's going to Iceland!'

Another body stung by the Icelandic bank meltdown was, er, the Metropolitan Police, who had £30 million invested. Amazingly, they had withdrawn all their funds on the advice of their treasurer, before putting it back in again. Clearly the Met should be spending less time surfing the Internet for once-in-a-lifetime savings deals and stick to what they do best: killing people.

Charities were also caught with their metaphorical cash pants down, to the tune of £120 million. But charities with huge cash reserves is a fucked-up idea anyway. Can't they just give the money to charity or something?

Peter Hepburn, the chief executive of Cats Protection, who banjaxed loads of their moggy money by shipping it out to Reykjavik, helped set up Save Our Savings (SOS), which represents thirty charities that had around £50 million deposited in Iceland. He accused the government of 'turning its back' on charities when it wouldn't bail them out.

But Alistair Darling just turned round and said: 'Look, mate, I've got a shitting meltdown on here. So fuck your cats, yeah?'

Celebrity survivalists

The future looks bleak. Fear is in the air. Even if capitalism holds up and we're not tearing each other up in the street like dogs, the environment will get us. Face it: we're going to be tearing each other up in the street like dogs. It's survival of the fittest. And, yes, that means celebrities.

First out of the traps is Neil Strauss, author of *The Game*, the bestselling guide to chatting up the ladies. 'A hot, rich, pampered intellectual with a big dick and a marathon tongue' (his words), ex-nerd Neil taught the world how to get pimped. Now he's getting pumped.

Emergency: One Man's Story of a Dangerous World and How to Stay Alive in It is his guide to post-meltdown survival.

'I don't want to be hiding in cellars, fighting old women for a scrap of bread, dying of cholera,' says Strauss. And on one level, who does?

Gearing up for meltdown involves going to see a man called Mad Dog to learn how to fashion a weapon by taping a razor blade to a credit card. Mad Dog is 'absolutely the man to see about knives', according to Strauss. In the past, people called Mad Dog who taught their children how to make weapons by taping together razor blades and credit cards were the sort of people to stay away from. Not any more . . .

The Honourable Kirstie Allsopp, meanwhile, built an entire cottage out of bits of spit and string she found in skips, all held together with a smidge of matronly gumption and wool. Kirstie is ready for the hard rain. Eagle-eyed viewers of Channel 4's *Kirstie's Homemade Home* will have noticed all the CCTV. And the moat. And the gun turrets. And the attack geese.

So the future is a bit like *I'm a Celebrity* . . . but not on telly (will there even be telly?) and in Wiltshire or somewhere. Or up a hill in Scotland. That's the best place to hole up in a post-apocalypse stockade – a remote Scottish farm with its own generator. Remote, lots of water and, er, not that I've been thinking about it much. Anyway . . .

Then there's Michael Portillo. Speaking on Radio 4, the pouty ex-Tory MP recalled the week of the banking collapse and the fears that everyone's money was about to disappear, saying, 'We seemed to be about a day away from *Lord of the Flies*.' Which for me provoked the image of Michael Portillo in short trousers, leading a gang of feral youths to stove a fat kid's head in with stones. Which is maybe slightly unfair really, because he isn't that sort of person at all. Not any more, anyway.

Or is dark Portillo now casting aside the veil? Shortly afterwards, he went to Bolivia and punched an elderly man right in the face. Filming the documentary *How Violent Are You?*, Portillo discovered that he is, apparently, quite violent. Violent enough to punch a man in the face, a man 'old enough to be his father'. Portillo's knuckles – the ones he hit the elderly man with – were bandaged in colourful straps as part of the traditional tribal costume of the Tinku fighting festival, a festival of fighting during which Portillo boned up on some fighting.

'I did get some satisfaction from knocking the man to the ground,' Portillo admitted. 'It's to do with the release of dopamine – the same powerful chemical reaction that makes us enjoy sex.'

Bloody hell, now I'm starting to see why Neil Strauss is so into societal breakdown – once you've knobbed hundreds of women, maybe fighting old people is the only thrill left in town.

Even George Monbiot's at it (not fighting oldies . . . not yet). Being the voice of environmental meltdown probably would slowly break your spirit, but when Monbiot starts asking readers of the *Guardian* if they've got a 'spare AK-47', you do have to wonder. And that's not the sort of question you can write off as rhetorical, is it? It's a straightforward request for readers of the *Guardian* newspaper to send in any surplus Russian assault rifles they have lying round the house. What could be more specific than that?

Strauss, Allsopp, Portillo, Monbiot . . . These brave few are the basis of the new master race. Perhaps Monbiot will vie for leadership with Portillo? It's Monbiot versus Portillo, for the future of humanity. Hard to say who will triumph in this clash. Portillo's bigger (and, as I say, can punch a man in the face), but Monbiot's got a gun.

Maybe they'll team up, like in a buddy movie. (Monbiot and Portillo – breakin' *all* the rules . . .) Anyway . . . I think we'll be all right as long as no one lets Strauss have the gun. That 'marathon tongue' of his will come in handy if they need to lick a lot of stamps (not that there will be any stamps), but he *must not be given the gun*. Ditto Allsopp: she'll only use it to force local tradespeople to fit new fabrics on to chairs she's found in skips: 'Who's the re-upholsterer now then, motherfucker!?' she might scream in their fear-stained faces. 'Why rent when you can buy? Why buy when you've got a gun!'

Of course, this is just worst-case scenario stuff.

Shami Chakrabarti's cultural life

The Director of Liberty, the National Council for Civil Liberties, is the ubiquitous justice campaigner always talking about justice. You've seen her on the news. She is probably on the news right now, as you are reading this. It's certainly possible. No one could criticise her work rate.

In fact, you could become concerned that she is working *too* hard. Particularly because, whenever she is asked about her general interests, she always relates them back somehow to justice and its evil nemesis, injustice. Shami Chakrabarti really hates justice's evil nemisis, injustice.

Ask her what's her favourite book and she will say *To Kill a Mockingbird* – Harper Lee's classic rumination on, er, justice. It's a good book and all, but is it Shami Chakrabarti's *favourite* book? Is it really?

Favourite film? *Twelve Angry Men*. Does the title refer to twelve angry vigilante men on a rampage? Not on your nelly. Favourite song of all time? Nina Simone's 'I Wish I Knew How It Would Feel to Be Free'. Apparently, she sang it to her baby – *every day*!

She can't even take her justice cap off when reading Harry Potter: '*The Order of the Phoenix* is all about human rights,' she once claimed. She's right, of course, the Ministry of Magic are bastards without a liberal bone in their bodies.

Things reached a head with this 'My Week' diary column that appeared in the *Observer*:

MONDAY
Got up and listened to the *Today* programme to see if there was anything about justice on it, or if anyone had been locked up in priz. There wasn't. Did some justice-related work, then went home and kicked back watching *Legal Eagles*, with Robert Redford and Debra Winger.

TUESDAY
Went to a conference about state power. The state really does have a lot of power. During the lunch break, I played 'I Fought the Law' on my iPod. He fought the law and the law won. It's so often the way.

WEDNESDAY

Long day at the office. Lots of people in priz this week. Like every week. Stay up late watching *Murphy's Law*. Jimmy Nesbitt is very good in it, but he doesn't always follow the rules to the letter. Must write to Jimmy Nesbitt about this. We cannot make exceptions. Jimmy Nesbitt of all people should know this.

THURSDAY

ID cards debate at Parliament. On the Tube, re-read *Crime and Punishment*. People should be punished for their crimes – it's people being punished without having committed any crimes that I can't stand. Luckily, the man being punished here had committed two major crimes.

FRIDAY

Debate Jon Gaunt about civil liberties. I pretend he's bringing something meaningful to the debate, but this is just a ploy to stop him swearing and pretending he's being silenced. Really I think he's an arsehole. Can't wait to get home and let my hair down. It's Friday night! And Friday night is '. . . And Justice for All' night. What Metallica don't know about justice isn't worth knowing.

SATURDAY

The weekend is here! Watch *Robin Hood* with the family. Can't help thinking that, with Toby Stephens' Prince John character, the BBC could be telling young people more about the importance of habeas corpus. Or we may all rue the consequences.

SUNDAY

Scan the Sunday papers for stuff about civil liberties being infringed. Watch Jim Jarmusch's *Down by Law*. Quite a disappointing amount of law in it.

Channel 4 cutting all programme budgets by 10 per cent

Let us pray that this does not lead to a rash of cheap, poorquality programming.

Hugo Chávez four-day TV spectaculars

Chavez has had his own weekly show, *Alo Presidente* ('Hello President'), since he was first elected President of Venezuela in 1999. It is shown on Sundays, from a different corner of the country each week.

Usually the format is a long talk about the evils of neoliberalism, including copious slating of critics and opponents, followed by the President singing a little song. He even sometimes phones up unsuspecting voters for a chat.

To mark his tenth anniversary in office, Chavez (who famously drinks a lot of coffee) decided to push the boat out. His previous record for a programme was a meagre eight hours, so he thought: Fuck it, I think I'll go on for four days.

And that's just too much Hugo Chavez for anyone. Even Chavez's most ardent supporters must look at the prospect of a four-day Hugo-a-thon and think, Shite on a bike! Absolutely not.

He planned to go through from Thursday to Sunday, doing anything up to ten hours a day, 'in chapters, like a soap opera', he explained. That's more than a fairly long long weekend. *Aloooooooooo Presidente!*

On the Thursday Chavez started well, giving sex education tips to a group of teenagers, and then talked about problems with his weight, which has ballooned since the former paratrooper first took office. Friday was also a winner, after he put in a call to his mentor Castro, who, as we know, is quite a laugh. And is also famous for brevity in his chitchat.

But on the Saturday, Chavez pulled the plug. Four days of non-stop Hugo Chavez was too much Hugo Chavez even for Hugo Chavez.

Venezuelans breathed a sigh of relief, and switched over to *Venezuela's Got Talent*. Which it has.

Christian theme parks

A weird Lancashire-based Christian charity backed by unnamed 'Christian businessmen' (whatever that means) is setting up a creationist theme park in the North-West of England. Which sounds like a hell of a day out, all in all.

Their aim is not just to give stoned students something to do during reading weeks, but to spread the word of Genesis. It's the theme park for people who think that other theme parks don't spread the word of Genesis enough. Thorpe Park? Almost entirely silent on the eternal struggle between heaven and hell. Although there is a ride called the Inferno. And as for

Legoland's assertion that the world is made of Lego – well, that's just silly isn't it, creationists?

Inspired by the 'Holy Land Experience' in Florida, the new park will include two cinemas, and a TV studio making family-oriented Christian programmes designed to lead youngsters out of the shadow of the valley of 'binge drinking'. There are also 3D cinematic holograms of biblical scenes. You would have to hope that Onan makes an appearance somewhere in there. Through all of this multi-media medievalism, the park's backers hope to bring an 'end to binge drinking'. They are obsessed with binge drinking: 'On television today there is so much sex and violence, it is no wonder our youth are binge drinking.' Binge drinking, binge drinking, binge drinking, and Jesus – it's all they seem to think about.

The Orlando park features an actual bloodied Jesus (an actor) carrying a cross while being flayed by Roman soldiers. Bizarrely, the mooted owners of the British park, AH Trust, don't plan to have one of those. Come on, AH Trust, Roman soldiers – *binge-drinking* Roman soldiers – flaying our Lord Jesus Christ? I reckon even I could lay off the pop for a couple of hours to watch that. Laying off the pop to watch binge-drinking Roman soldiers flaying our Lord Jesus Christ – that's me, that is.

Anyway, the kids will love it! Well, they'd better. With God on board, you'd expect it to be an improvement on Alton Towers. If it's not better than Alton Towers, there is no God.

By the way, the AH Trust originally wanted to put its remarkable theme park on the site of a closed-down B&Q in Wigan (poignant). But spokesperson Peter Jones (not the one off *Dragons' Den*) explained: 'Wigan Council slammed the door in our faces. You mention the C word, and people don't want to know.'

Well, there was no need to be rude.

Church of England

Anglicans? Waste of space.

Asked who or what was to blame for the recession, Archbishop of Canterbury Rowan Williams joked: 'I was going to suggest Satan.'

But why joke about it? If that's what you think, just fucking spit it out!

'It was Beelzebub lurking in you all! You're all going to burn!' That kind of thing. Come on, you're a man of God! You don't have to be reasonable about anything. It's one of the perks of the job!

But no. When asked whether the crisis was beneficial, Williams replied: 'It is a sort of a reality check, isn't it – which is always good for us.'

Rather than the obvious retort: 'It's a reckoning! A reckoning for cavorting with the Horned One!' Come on, man, are you still in this game or what? Never mind political Islam, even the Catholics have got an anti-gay Pope who used to be a Nazi.

A measure of quite how hopeless the Church of England is at religion is that even Richard Dawkins really likes the C of E: 'Oh, Rowan Williams – what a sweet man!' he exclaimed to Rosie Millard. 'I have a lot of time for the Church of England . . . If all Christians were like Rowan, there wouldn't be a problem. I've met him socially, and he's delightful.'

Are you having this, Williams? Because if he's not doing Satan's work, I don't know who is. He's the guy who goes round getting literally red in the face because of God. If you asked him, 'Do you think God is bollocks?', he would say, 'Yes, I do think God is bollocks.' Go on – excommunicate him or something. Smite the fucker down!

Cityboy memoirs

For a Cityboy, writing a Cityboy memoir is a bit like being one of the MPs who got in early and gave cheques back at the start of the expenses scandal. It's seeing the way the wind is blowing and wanting to say loud and proud and clear: 'Not me! *Them*. Hate them. I never even wanted to work there in the first place. Well, not much.'

Anyway, now the blizzard of cocaine has become a blizzard of insider books, blowing the lid on all sorts of nefarious – and preferably saucy (if you want to sell any copies) – goings-on in the City, Tokyo, etc.

Here we have assembled a cut-out-and-keep guide to writing your very own Cityboy memoir. You just order the pieces in any random way you like and, through the magic of words, they will still add up to some book sales if you put the words 'DRUGS' and 'SEX' on the cover. Oh, and they'll obviously also provide a comprehensive insight into life inside the Golden Mile. Like, totally.

- So I got a job in the City. I didn't really want to. But I did. Etc.

- I'm not the sort who normally works there. I'm much better than that. Etc.
- But I definitively did work there though, so I do know what was going on. So this is definitely the sort of book where you can pretend you've learned something, even though it is mostly about DRUGS and SHAGGING and STRIPPERS. Etc.
- My first boss was Dave. He was a nutter. But what he didn't know about whatever it is we were supposed to be doing wasn't worth knowing. Even though Dave used to steal everyone's commission off them, I respected him. He was a total, total cunt, but his girlfriend was a stripper. She had great tits. I saw them and everything. Well, I say girlfriend, but she left him after that time he wet himself again.
- Then there was Jamie. He was a right cunt, but he taught me everything there is to know about pretending to know everything there is to know about futures, whatever the fuck they are. (I do actually know, I'm just trying to sound cool.) After a few lagers and sambucas – like, fucking twenty, yeah? – he was a right sharp one. 'Look at the fucking hooters on that!' he'd shout. Stuff like that. He was a true friend. Even though, as I say, he was the one who got me sacked.
- Then there was Phil. It was Phil who told me the secret to being able to sleep with strippers: having lots of money. You won't get to sleep with strippers much – they aren't stupid – but his plan was still the best one on the table. 'You can't sleep with all the strippers all of the time,' he said. 'But you

can sleep with some of the strippers some of the time.' He was full of wise words like that. 'Even if it's only, like, once,' he added, 'it's still worth the expense.'

- 'And if all else fails and you really just don't get to sleep with any strippers at all – like, not even one,' he went on, 'just go to a whore. They *can't* say no. Well, they can, and they sometimes do. But it's definitely more straightforward.'

- Talking to a room full of people about energy price forecasts when you've BEEN ON DRUGS LOOKING AT STRIPPERS FOR THREE DAYS is quite difficult to pull off. You probably knew that already, deep down. BUT I'VE ACTUALLY DONE IT. (Given a presentation, that is – not strippers. Although I HAVE DEFINITELY SLEPT WITH SOME STRIPPERS.)

Then just throw in some random stuff about how having to privatise the orphanage you grew up in made you see the light. It definitely, *definitely*, wasn't the looming recession and prospect of almost inevitable unemployment that motivated you to jump ship. Fictionalise if you want, giving strippers codenames. And remember: you were only doing what anyone would have done in your position. The system is to blame. Etc. Put in a few diagrams off the back of an envelope – to show, quite literally, how you used to make up investment plans on the back of an envelope. Make up the acronyms if you want to, but do put in plenty of details about the strippers. I can't stress that enough.

Pretend you're a gardener now or something, or work with kids in the inner city, or you're going to set up a commune. The key phrases here are 'gnawing emptiness', 'more to life than strippers' and 'give something back'.

Although when using 'give something back', make it absolutely clear you don't mean the money. Ker-ching!

Cityboy teachers

On one level, skilled men and women exchanging their old lives of selfish acquisition for one of public service should be seen as a good thing. And certainly the Training and Development Agency has had a good recession, gleefully hoovering up ex-City types to plug holes in maths and science teaching. Well, they do have some good war stories to liven up the classes . . .

'Sir, tell us about the time you brought down the yen!'

'Yeah, go on, sir!'

'Oh, you don't want to hear about all that *again*. Do you?'

And their real-world experience will also enliven lesson activities by introducing more practical aspects.

'So, if some bloke in Bongo Bongo Land's got twelve beans, and I take ten of the beans and give him twelve dollars, but I also lend him another twelve dollars at twenty-eight per cent APR – that's APR, mind – then I sign the beans over to the American subsidiary, then to Japan, then back to me on a lend–lease basis, how many beans have I got?'

'Er, ten, sir?'

'Wrong again, Symonds! You're forgetting the offshore beans that – altogether now . . .'

'NO ONE NEEDS TO KNOW ABOUT, SIR!'

'Precisely. Now, who's got the coke?'

'Davis, sir.'

'Safe.'

Coca-Cola doing deals with the devil

You'd have thought Coke would have been more careful about who they associate with. Having already been accused of complicity in the murder of trade unionists by death squads at bottling plants in Colombia, benefiting from the use of child labour in Salvadorean sugar plantations, exposing Indian workers to water shortages and contaminated water, and so on, their reputation was not exactly spotless. Then they went one worse: they got into bed with Innocent Smoothies.

Yes. Those bastards. The cutesy-cutesy fruit-crushing crushing bores, with their mimsy oh-so-friendly hilarious marketing. I mean, for fuck's sake, Coca-Cola, what are you fucking doing to yourselves?

I jest, of course. It's Coca-Cola who are the bastards and Innocent who are the goodies. When news emerged that Coca-Cola had bought a £30 million stake in the notorious smoothie company, Innocent founder Richard Reed explained: 'This might not initially sound right, but it is right . . .'

Cool.

'In some small ways,' he continued, 'we may be able to influence their thinking.'

Cool. Just don't wait in for a reply to those emails though, eh?

Perhaps they should add on to their smoothie cartons, alongside the pictures of a coconut ('we've included one of these') and bananas ('and two of these . . .'), a little picture of a dead trade unionist ('. . . and none of these!').

Anyway, let's hope it all pans out better than Coke's last great UK venture. You know, when they bottled 'purified' tap water and sold it. Cunts.

Cool camping

While everyone else is still sweltering in the city, you and yours are getting your heads together in the country. Not in one of those everything-pegged-out-neatly campsites that smell of paraffin either, but a cool campsite. Not grannies in statics watching Westerns. God, not that. Acoustic guitars, though.

Okay, so the toilets are rubbish and have a slippy floor. But you can pitch up where you like and the owner comes round with firewood and sits down to tell you about Mayans and stuff. And, yes, there is some cock-monkey bashing his bongos at 4 a.m., but it's cool. It's cool camping.

Obviously, the coolest campsites, the ones that people stand around duck ponds and whisper about, are booked up for years in advance. But you can still go to a quite cool campsite and that will be, you know, cool. But I wonder what happens when your designated night under cool canvas finally rolls round, and your Shangri-La turns out actually to be a field? A nice field, with trees around, but still, nonetheless, a field? And it's raining? Don't worry, it's great. Cool campers only have great times.

Granted, if you are extremely fortunate, camping in Britain can be a pleasant enough experience – but it's never *ever* going to be 'cool'. Even if Beth Ditto was on board, it would still only be fucking camping. In a fucking tent. In a fucking campsite. Camping is one of the very few things it is chemically impossible to infuse with some sense of smug superiority. Even a yurt's just a tent!

Sorry about that. That was a terrible thing to say.

It sort of is, though.

Co-operative Bank

Business is booming at the Co-op due to its position as the 'ethical bank', untainted by coke-driven investment madness orgies. They even have adverts featuring baskets of eggs, which should tell you everything you need to know.

But is the Co-op really so good? Is it, really? Has anyone actually looked into it? I mean, you wouldn't bank on their ready meals being, in any way whatsoever, good. There was something distinctly unethical about one curry I had from there, so who says they're any better with money?

Okay, it's better than the Spar. This much I freely admit. But no one's going to entrust their savings to, say, Londis, so why should this be any different?

Because it's a bank? Yeah, well, that's what they would say, isn't it? It sounds convenient, but we've all been burned with this kind of shit now. And that's why I bank with Budgens. You should too. They open late. And they sell tinnies. The fact that they don't claim to be a bank is all to the good. Say I sent you.

Credit crunch horse murder

When's that pony going to grow up and get a proper job? That's the question on a lot of lips these days. As it turns out, horses are pretty pricey. Well, they are big buggers. (Even the small ones are fairly big.)

Since recession hit, the Horse Trust, a Chilterns rest home for retired mules, horses and donkeys, has been 'deluged' with calls from owners desperate to find a new home for their pets. But, according to a report in the *Mail*: 'Unfortunately, the Trust has no magic solution; only a final one.'

So it's like the Holocaust down there, but for horses.

'Look, in times of plentiful credit, my angel, I was very happy for you to revel in a love of nature, maybe coming to love that beautiful, sweet white pony of yours as you might a sibling. Dear old Mrs Magoo. She's a good girl, Mrs Magoo. But that was then and this is now, and sadly we do have to shoot her. *Right* in the face.'

But what *is* the best way to kill a horse? It's a question we all face sooner or later. An injection is often preferred, although some argue this merely benefits the owner; that it's the instant hit – the bullet – that the horse would actually prefer. If it was able to express a preference.

'It's not a pleasant thing, it never is,' said Trust chief Brigadier Paul Jepson. 'It's harrowing for the owners to have to watch because it appears violent. There's a big bang, the horse collapses to the ground, and then, even though it's dead, its body shakes a bit. After that, the carcass is winched up and placed on a truck.'

Yes, that does appear violent. So there we have it: killing a horse is violent. We probably knew that already, deep down, but it's good to have it confirmed by a military man.

Once your horse is dead, it can be sold on for dogs to eat or, sometimes, to the French (to eat). 'A fellmonger charges about £250 or more to shoot the horse and take it away,' says Jess Winchester of HorseWorld. 'A vet charges £60–80 to deliver a lethal injection, but then you would still have the responsibility for disposing of the body.'

One cheap option could involve getting a vet in, then seeing if friends or neighbours can help you carry the carcass to the nearest hunt kennel. That has to be the thriftiest option here. If, you know, grim.

Anyway, something else to add to the bleak-future list: death camps for ponies.

D

Darling's commie budget

Media reaction to Alistair Darling's shit-or-bust May 2009 budget gave the lie to the so-called death of ideology and convergence of politics at the centre. Suddenly the right was up and about and everywhere, stamping up and down on the vengeful assassin of the left, which it said (screamed) had just jumped out from behind the curtain where it had been lurking, patiently, since 1997. Yes, it was class war. And Alistair Darling had started it.

Darling had used all the tools in his armoury to disguise his deep inner purposes. But not even his key skill of speaking monotonously while also not moving his face much could hide the fact that, yes, he was going to raise tax a bit on the small minority of people who earn over £150,000 a year.

This move prompted reactions of: 'I knew it! I knew that New Labour was just a front. The twelve years of privatisations, the tax breaks for the rich – it was all just a put-on. *Now* they bare their teeth, the Trotskyite scum! Look at them! They've been waiting for this moment all their lives! Flee to the hills! Move abroad! Move to hills, abroad! Hide inside hilltop fortresses made of steel!'

The Times illustrated the point with an illustration –

a huge cartoon of Alistair Darling's face, with his eyebrows coloured in, in red, like two angry wee commie beasties. 'RED ALL OVER' screamed the headline. It all made so much sense now. How did people not realise he was a red, red all over? What with his eyebrows being red?

Okay, he'd been pretty cunning in hiding his inherent hard-left tendencies by basically never doing anything left-wing ever before, or even now in fact. But think about it: how cunning is *that*?

It was hard-hitting stuff from *The Times*. Or was it childish? Bearing in mind that their response featured 'colouring in' as a major plank, possibly the latter.

Attacking Darling's optimistic growth forecasts, the *Mail*'s illustrators went one further, showing ALISTAIR IN WONDERLAND, dressed in a blue-and-white Alice dress with flowing – quite fetching, actually – blond locks, being assailed by aggressive playing cards. (Do *you* have psychedelic Alistair Darling dreams? I do.) Inside, the massed writers roared: 'Once again the rich are to be soaked . . . backbone of wealth creation . . . brain drain . . . sick man of Europe . . .'

Okay, so massive public borrowing will mean public sector carnage to come – unlikely to go down in history as overly 'red'. But at times like these, it's not ourselves we should be feeling for – it's the high-earners, the income group all the journalists want to join. The politics/business/media establishment whose brains got us in this mess in the first place. If those bastards fuck off, we'll be sick men! Even the women! Do you want that? Europe laughing at us? *Laughing* because we've got no brains or backbone and we're all brain-dead and sick and they're not? I can't see the problem myself, but for the *Mail* it's a big issue.

The *Sun* tried to look on the bright side: 'AT LEAST IT'S SUNNY' it screamed, over a picture of some deckchairs on a pebbly beach. In a banner at the top, though, sad-face emoticons were sad. The forlorn yellow faces were sad about 2p on petrol. And sad about the £175 billion of new public debt.

The *Express*, which is increasingly like a copy of *Chat* magazine that's had too much coffee, wasn't sidetracked by the weather and roared: 'THEY'VE RUINED BRITAIN'. The *Financial Times* stuck to old-school news values on the front page – 'Darling gambles on growth' – but spoiled it a little with an editorial inside entitled 'What a cheeky fucker'. 'I knew it!' began the editorial . . .

So, generally, the reaction wasn't positive.

Death of J.G. Ballard

It's interesting that, just when everyone started going on about a bloated and alienated consumer culture collapsing under its own weight, and people eating each other and setting up alternative societies in overgrown abandoned shopping centres and the repressed beast within unleashing itself and everyone, like, fucking cars in a sex way and living on boats that float on swamps where the M25 used to be and all that, the novelist J.G. Ballard, for some fifty years the prophet of a bloated and alienated consumer culture collapsing under its own weight and people eating each other and all that, took the precaution of dying.

It *could* have been a coincidence, you know? But, really, deep down, does anyone actually believe that? And if things are too Ballardian for J.G. Ballard, then that's certainly too Ballardian for me. And I speak as somebody who finds quite a lot of his books too Ballardian, so I definitely don't want it happening outside my front window.

Donations to charity shops going through the floor

Charity shops should be doing okay. People are looking for stuff in charity shops – *Lonely Planet* guides, mug trees . . . They're just not finding stuff in charity shops. Because no one is giving stuff to charity shops.

'This trend might gain a momentum of its own and charity shops will have nothing to sell,' warned David Moir of the Association of Charity Shops. Fucking hell – not *another* apocalypse. Maybe the Association of Charity Shops will have to be renamed the Association of Charity Shops with Fuck-All to Sell.

What's going on here? How did even that part of the system break down? Charity shops are what open when other shops close. But now the charity shops are becoming charity cases.

Somewhere out there, someone must be thinking: 'You know what? I won't give that copy of *Pablo Honey* to charity. I might need it later . . . you know, for trading. And that tea tray, you could make a hut with that, or a weapon.'

Doom and gloom for billionaires

The billionaires had been doing fairly well before the crash, what with being billionaires. With the fetters on wealth accumulation gone, they were free to increase their pickings tenfold, until the richest five hundred people had more wealth than half the world's population – the poorest three billion. The super-rich had to invent new and inventive ways to spend their money, to the point where some observers claimed they sort of lived in their own country, Richistan: a place where butlers, fresh from the raft of new butler schools, know how to get you Chunky Monkey ice cream at midnight in the Mediterranean. That's the life, eh?

But then the *Sunday Times* Rich List 2009 made for ugly reading. For billionaires. Lakshmi Mittal's fortune had dropped from £17 billion to £10.8 billion and Richard Branson's from £1.5 billion to £1.2 billion. In just a year, the overall numbers of billionaires in Britain had fallen from 75 to 43. Yes, billionaire numbers were in decline. There was some serious billionaire endangerment going on. The headline 'Bonfire of the Billionaires' said it all: a funeral pyre – with billionaires on top. A flaming stack of burning billionaires. Bet you're feeling sorry now, aren't you? Bastard.

Although how much 'doom and gloom for billionaires' was there really? I don't know, but I half-suspect they're still basically doing all right. And Donald Trump agrees with me, as he sometimes does. Speaking on behalf of his supposedly beleaguered class, he insisted: 'We're not going down, we're going up. We're buying things we couldn't have dreamed of buying two years ago.'

Well, thank the fucking stars for that. And, if a few billions have disappeared here and there, they had generally remembered to put something aside for a rainy day. Indeed, after Bear Stearns' hedge funds went down the toilet, head honcho Jimmy Cayne admitted: 'I just got my ass kicked. But I was almost dispassionate . . . the only people who are going to suffer are my heirs, not me. Because when you have a billion six, and you lose a billion, you're not exactly like crippled, right?'

Indeed not. Even so, I still do worry for them. Or, more particularly, for their heirs. Look at the history: given free rein of unearned wealth, it's a racing cert they will all become preening fuck-ups who end up gambling/overdosing/doing sex tapes, etc. Is that what you want? Where's your humanity?

Clearly, we need to extract the billions from the billionaires painlessly, for the sake of the children. They'll thank us for it eventually. But how? These new times require new thinking, and so we ourselves have set up a think-tank for just this purpose. It's called The Centre for Is It Just Me or Has the Shit Hit the Fan Studies and here are our preliminary thinkings:

1. Send the super-rich into space (they like that sort of thing), then take their money away, and when they come back, say, 'Sorry, we don't know what happened, we were out.'

2. Sell it to them as an efficiency saving: we could put your riches towards greening the global economy, the alternative being the unravelling of all human society on earth, which might have hidden costs. You never know, these people might go for it. They hate hidden costs.

3. Get Paul McKenna to write a book for the super-

rich called *I Can Make You Even Richer*, with a big picture of Paul McKenna on the front. Give them all copies, they follow it to the letter not realising that it's all a cunning ruse – it's actually going to make them far poorer! (NOTE: Check with McKenna – would he be into this?)

4. Start a new TV show called *What Is to Be Done About a Problem Like the Super Rich?* and pretend everyone text-voted for them to give away all their money.

5. Give the super-rich a big new island – they like islands. Tell them we're going to send on their money later. Then never send it.

6. Cast a spell to send them to sleep for a hundred years and surround their castles with a thick, thorny hedge. Raid their funds and put it towards, say, sorting out the global water supply. If the spell doesn't work, try Xanax or ketamine?

Anyway, when we put this up on the Internet, to great fanfare, some wag blogged at the bottom: 'Why not tax them?' Which just makes a fantasy-mockery of the whole thing. Well, maybe we could give that a go, if the whole thorny-castle thing doesn't pan out . . .

Dramas portraying Margaret Thatcher as a sexy lady

Thatcher is never off the telly these days, and not just all those references on the news. For as the illusion of deregulated free-market prosperity shatters to dust and becomes a joke of almost cosmic proportions, one's thoughts do often turn to the former Prime Minister. Not in a frisky way, though.

The timely dramatisations of Margaret Thatcher's life are fine up to a point, but is there not a danger in casting notably easy-on-the-eye actresses like Andrea Riseborough and Lindsey Duncan in the lead role? Might younger viewers not assume that our former leader was, well, quite sexy? When, in reality, this WASN'T THE CASE AT ALL? Okay, some people thought she was sexy. But these people had wrong minds. (Alan Clark apparently used to sit behind Thatch in Parliament getting off on her ankles. Mucky toff bastard.)

The Road to Finchley even suggested that Thatch once tried to have it off with Ted Heath, for fuck's sake. Who are they going to get for the drama-doc on the Falklands: Jessica Alba?

Bob Dylan, Worship of recent works by

Across the board, it's 5/5 for Bob Dylan's new album. Apparently, it's a riot. 'Turn the record up real loud and shake this mama one more time,' said *Uncut*.

One live show in Cardiff was called 'an awe-inspiring process to witness, one of the few surviving wonders of the Great American Experiment, as enduring in its own way as Mount Rushmore, *Citizen Kane* or Charlie Chaplin', and a BBC news report about his first US number-one album since 1970 said this was despite his last three albums 'being the most critically acclaimed of his career'. *Not* the 60s ones, the 90s–00s ones.

Christ on a bike, I thought, this late-Dylan shit must be *good*. The unravelling of Western capitalism must have really inspired the old boy. He must have really shown those bastards what for, galvanised a new vision of hope for America and the world, maybe socking it to the military-industrial war-mongers, more rampant even than before, perhaps delivering shards of surrealist poetry to mirror the tumult of our dreams, deliver some exhortations to rouse the youth from its slumbers . . .

Actually, though, it's loads of bar-blues about feeling well old. 'Ooh, I'm feelin' old . . . Still feelin' old/Hard to make it up the stairs . . .' It's mainly like that.

Getting darker, is it? Oh dear. Sorry about that. Feels like the world's moving on and leaving you behind? Well, yes. Being old not as good as being young? Thought not. For fuck's sake, I can get all this from my gran. She doesn't make any fucking sense either.

He is a good DJ, though. Maybe *he* should take over the Radio 1 breakfast show. ('And the times they are a-just coming up to seven-thirty . . .') Chris Moyles ranting about losing his job to Bob Dylan? I think I would like to hear that.

'Who is Bob Dylan anyway? I mean, how many awards has *he* got?'

E

Eastern Europe looking like Eastern Europe again

If you're thinking you're having a bad economic crisis, check out Hungary – the economy only being kept afloat by billions in IMF loans, Nazi militias on the street and, to make matters worse, there's a goalkeeper in charge.

Gordon Bajnai, a former goalkeeper for the 43rd Epitok, a fourth-division side, became Prime Minister in April 2009. He was presumably chosen, if only subliminally, for connotations of 'safe hands'. Although he's not that safe: he's also known as 'Goose Gordon' for his role in a high-profile poultry farm scheme that went tits up. (High-profile poultry farm schemes? Crazy guys.) He is also a former Economy Minister, I'll admit that; he's not just a *random* goalkeeper. But he *is* a goalkeeper.

They'll be needing some safe hands, what with the uni-formed paramilitary troops, organised by the black-shirted Magyar Garda/Hungarian Guard movement, marching in Nazi regalia and flying wartime Fascist Party flags, attacking Roma homes and social democrat politicians, and generally purveying anti-Semitic propaganda.

It's not isolated either – all across Eastern Europe, it's basically up with paramilitary skinheads marching about the place, down with boutiques and coffee shops.

To say these populations were victims of misselling when they were promised a slice of the pie/Western Dream if they signed up for the neo-con project of privatise, liberalise and borrow shitloads of cash, is to do a vast disservice to ordinary, decent missellers. Turns out that slashing welfare programmes actually *increases* poverty! Who'd have thought it? All told, the market fundamentalists could not have done a better job of knacking over Eastern Europe if they had tried. Or maybe they *did* try.

Either way, it certainly looks like the region is now properly finding out what it means not to have won the Cold War. There are pitched battles between farmers and plain-clothes police officers in Latvia. Factories in Romania relocating to *even lower-wage* economies. Putin shipping out Moscow riot police to quell car-worker protests . . .

Still, don't panic too much. A goalkeeper in charge and Nazi militias on the street? For Britain, I'd say that's at least two years away.

Economists

Someone once said that an economist is 'someone who can tell you tomorrow why they were wrong yesterday'. Recent events would seem to suggest this is a wildly optimistic assessment of their skills.

Seriously, try it out. Go and ask an economist: 'Why were you wrong yesterday?' They won't have a fucking clue.

El Cruncho

Spanish for 'the crunch'. Possibly.

Many Brits emigrating to Spain thought they were going to El Dorado. But they soon found they were in El Shit. There was no work anywhere. Crash-hit natives were becoming more restive. Falling interest rates nixed planned incomes. The pound just wasn't even trying. And according to Debbie, recently relocated from Harrogate to the Costa Del Sol: 'The cost of living was astronomical. The only things that are really cheap there are cigs and booze but you can't live on them.'

Can't live on cigs and booze? Are you sure you're properly throwing yourself into the expat lifestyle there?

It's now got so bad that some people who have been in Spain for decades are returning to Britain, of all places. The British Embassy in Spain has posted on its website tips for those planning on returning to the old country after a long break, warning about social changes like satellite television, supermarket cashback, no NHS dentists. Other tips include:

- You will find people to be more caffeinated than you could ever have imagined. Not Nescafé. Really strong stuff, by the pint. It will blow your minds.
- There's loads of programmes on TV about people moving to Spain. For some reason.

- The people of Hartlepool voted in a pantomime monkey as Mayor. Four years later, they re-elected him.
- The Millennium Dome is now a big success. This was achieved by changing its name.
- Bruce Forsyth is still on the television. This might shock you, but it is something UK residents completely accept. Bruce Forsyth is *still* on the television. Perhaps he will always be on the television.
- There are no shops in Rotherham any more.
- Sven-Göran Eriksson is being paid a million pounds a year by League Two club (that's Fourth Division to you) Notts County.
- Esther Rantzen reckons she's going to be an MP.
- Lots of people have tans, but not nut-brown tans like yours, more orangey-brown. Your suspicions are correct: they are FAKE.
- Look, you know what? Don't go back. It's weird there. Stay where you are. What? They spit at you in the street? It doesn't matter.

Electric cars, Noises for

Electric cars make very little noise, which can take some getting used to. Okay, you might think that you'd get used to it. But no, you won't have the chance. Electric cars are to be fitted with a simulated petrol-engine-style 'growl', apparently.

This will be a legal requirement. The amplifier will be wired to the accelerator pedal so you can rev your electric car.

Whatever. Blind people in particular have expressed concern about how they will know if an electric car is coming, so whatever. It does seem something of a missed opportunity to give the cars a more interesting noise, though. Dub reggae, for example, or classic ska – with a toaster intermittently booming, 'Easy now!'

Eminem

Cooeee!
Guess who!
Go on, guess . . .
You know you want to!
Do you want a clue?
You don't need a clue, do you?
Yes, that's right,
You knew who it was all along,
It's Eminem (the rapper),
I'm back,
I heard you missed me,
Well, now I'm back,
It is right you missed me, isn't it?
That's what I got told,
I hope I haven't been misinformed,
So, basically, just wanted to say that really,
As I say, I am back,
I should be around a lot more from now on,
So if you need me for any reason . . .
I mean, I do have some stuff on,
I'm not saying I'll be able to drop everything just like that,

But I'll definitely be more available,
More than before,
Anyway, gotta dash,
Not going far, though . . .

(FADE)

Enron story being taken as a 'how-to' guide

If only we could have had some kind of warning about
what happens when you push capitalist madness to the
point where all the wheels have fallen off and you are
careering along on the chassis, sparks flying everywhere
while whooping, 'Woah, man! Look at all the sparks!' You
know, another one. *Apart* from Enron.

Donate to political buddies to cut all regulation, hide
troubling losses in a bewildering series of subsidiary companies, badmouth anyone who suspects this is all a house
of cards . . . just some of the nuggets we learned about the
collapse of Enron in 2001. And the business world seems to
have taken the story as a lesson not in how *not* to do things,
but in how *to do* things.

There was even a film, *Enron: The Smartest Guys in the
Room*. But the title was ironic! They thought they were the
smartest guys in the room, but they weren't! They were the
guys in the room closest to the biggest fuck-off fraud case
in US legal history. Is that smart? Is it fucking fuck.

Did they just watch the bits about the strippers and
rugged thousand-mile Mexican dirt-bike trips and then fall
asleep before the psychological collapse, fraud charges and

suicides? Then wake up as the credits rolled thinking: Well, it all worked out well for those guys . . .?

A lesson for us all then: always watch DVDs all the way through. Let's hope they never rent, say, *Deliverance*.

Enviro-apocalypse product opportunism

That toy, Road Rippers' RECYCLE TODAY – SAVE TOMORROW recycling truck, may, in some strange way, raise awareness – albeit among very small children, who probably shouldn't be aware of that shit anyway.

But – and this is the point – it is plastic and was made in China and has been transported all the way from China. And how exactly is that 'helping'?

Extended financial families

'This is a bigger financial event than any of us have lived through,' says Phillip Hodson from the British Association for Counselling and Psychotherapy. 'It's also an existential crisis.'

This is particularly true if you have to move back in with your parents. I'm feeling more lost and alone in a heartless, pointless world just thinking about it.

'Extended financial families' are growing exponentially. Not just kids moving back in with parents, but everyone moving back in with everyone. Moving back in with family members they've barely even met before! Now *that's* familial.

These are some stories from the extended financial front-line:

Clare, 31, shares with her ex

After five happy years, me and Mike realised that we were incompatible in every way. But we couldn't sell the flat, and Mike got laughed at for asking about another mortgage. So we decided to have a second life together – as flatmates. It's interesting . . . a bit awkward when we bring other people back. Maybe if we'd bought a *two*-bedroomed flat . . .

Hannah, 32, shares flat with her brother

I was never that close with Tom before, but now I really feel like I know him almost too well. Yes, I do get fed up when he plays the drums in the night. But, hey, we're on the property ladder – and that's what counts. I do like having a man around. It's all about security. Even though Tom often leaves the front door open. I've asked him about it, but he can't see the problem. He's like that, Tom. He's great.

Dave, 19, moved in with his gran

I bought a house with my gran. I thought, like, woah! All those biscuits, man, and games of Animal Snap. And she's not all that dopey – she knew I'd nicked some of her Valium almost immediately. I didn't care, though, because I was off my face. Old people love jellies. And if you come in drunk you can go up on the stairlift. So I was well into moving in with Gran. But it turned into a complete disaster. Meals on Wheels kept waking me up. And then Gran died, and everyone got on to me because I didn't notice and then my cousins split half the house between them, only they couldn't agree what to do with it so they put up, like, eight partition walls and rented the spaces out as really tiny flats. So I wouldn't buy a house with my gran again. Not even the other gran. The one who's not dead. She's in a home anyway. They won't let me live there. I asked.

F
―

Failure of Grant Bovey's buy-to-let empire making you wonder whether markets are just after all, The

I have never been a great one for the idea of a pure market where quality succeeds and shoddiness falters. Being that it just never seems to pan out that way in practice. Not even, you know, once. But then Grant Bovey goes down and you think: Hey, maybe there's something in this market stuff after all. It's enough to shake an entire belief system, watching a house of mirrors crash round the ears of one single Grant Bovey.

In April 2008, Bovey threatened to sue anyone who said he and celebrity wife Anthea Turner were in financial trouble: 'I am sitting in our £5m chateau in the Alps,' he thundered. 'I will sue anyone who says [buy-to-let company] Imagine Homes is in financial difficulty . . . [We] have huge profits that are yet to materialise.'

Sadly, those profits always remained more spiritual than corporeal in nature and, by Christmas, Imagine Homes (presumably as in 'Imagine it's in profit') had been taken over by HBOS (and if HBOS were a better bet in late 2008, you really were fucked).

Imagine Furnishings, meanwhile, had also gone to the

wall (along with various other Bovey companies called Imagine), and Bovey was admitting that most of the couple's £100 million paper fortune had turned to dust. As the golden couple told the media, there was a distinct possibility they could lose 'our mansion', set in a fifty-seven-acre Surrey estate, complete with polo field, stables and cinema. Weeping, literally weeping, Anthea lamented: 'Our backs are against the wall.' (Even then, she couldn't not point out that their house was a 'mansion' – even when they might lose 'our mansion'.)

These were the crisis days, the eye of the storm, and there was the very real possibility there would need to be a state bailout of Grant Bovey, with the taxpayer taking a major stake in Grant Bovey. It really was that bad. Was Grant Bovey 'too big' to be allowed to fail? That was the question.

Estimates put the unpaid business debts of Bovey's ventures at £28 million. But he was back in action within weeks with a new company – one buying up other people's distressed assets, the Distressed Property Company Limited. What a cool idea. This did piss off the creditors from when he wound up his other firms, though, all £28 million of them. But, hey, in a way, weren't these just small-minded people getting in the way of a dream? That's the way I look at it. No, hang on, not me: him. That's the way *he* looks at it.

Anthea, drawing on those common-touch skills honed on the GMTV sofa, likes to draw out the human cost: 'Those people who moan about you driving around in your nice big car are forgetting that the guy who washes the car now hasn't got a job.'

Don't you see this is hurting the little man here?!?! As if really to draw out this point, Turner and Bovey made sure they hurt the little man, to illustrate just how much the little man was being hurt by all this. 'I could have lost my business,' said Dawn Shields, director of a cleaning company sitting on an unpaid £7800 bill.

Then of course there's all the money they took out of the businesses (the ones that went bust owing people a lot of money) – some £4 million over three years. Imagine Furnishings posted a loss of close to £700,000 in 2006. But in 2007 Anthea was paid a consultancy fee of £389,410, plus an advance of £240,792. Oh, and her interest-free loan of £537,738 was written off.

Really, though, are Grant and Anthea comfortable with all this? I mean, yeah, they did put themselves about the media bewailing their misfortune, looking to all the world about as natural as they will ever manage to look. But do you think that either Grant Bovey or Anthea Turner – human beings, after all, 'victims of the credit crunch', just like everyone else – could look those creditors in the eye? Really look them in the eye, square in the eye, ball to ball, without blinking, without even feeling a touch of human shame?

You know, I actually think they could. No bother.

Alex Ferguson going on for ever

When Manchester United won the Premiership title for the third time on the trot – equalling Liverpool's record of eighteen top-flight titles – all United manager Sir Alex Ferguson could do was look to the future. What with him being only sixty-seven and everything.

The prospect of winning more titles 'resonated' with him, he said. He was vibrating – pulsating even – with the insatiable inner need for more, more, more.

The uncompromising Scottish footballing behemoth declared: 'I hope to win it another 83 times precisely – if I manage to live until I'm 150. That's the way it is in the modern game – you have to live until you're 150.

'Ryan Giggs'll still be up and down that wing like a nipper, eh? He'll only be 118 when I'm 150. Closing the gap, eh? Credit to the game. Great club. Etc.

'And will the wee man live that long? Your man there. Rafa Benítez? Will he live that long? Will he fuck. What an arsehole.'

The Ferguson–Benítez rumble had grumbled on all season, with Benítez's Liverpool responding to Man Utd's dominance with some interesting tactics. Not on the football pitch – in their own heads. Indeed, on the pitch Liverpool yet again forgot that an important part of the increasingly demanding modern game is to beat other teams who are not as good at football as you are, at football, on a fairly regular basis, if not weekly, and sometimes on Tuesday nights as well. This fatal flaw in their otherwise impressive footballing armoury was to cost them dear yet again.

Despite Liverpool going top for a spell earlyish in the season, United had Liverpool firmly in their wake long before the home straight. Gamely, Liverpool kept 'chasing' – a telling word, in that it basically means 'following'. 'From behind.' But they never, ever gave up. 'Erm, we've just got to keep going and hope United slip up, la,' said Jamie Carragher, or Steven Gerrard, or one of them anyway. The ultimate professionals, their dogged-ness was a credit to the game, etc. etc., blah blah, etc. If futile.

Well, it was not – ever – futile to Liverpool, who refused to give up even when Man Utd had actually won. Asked to congratulate Ferguson after a 0–0 draw with Arsenal saw United crowned champions, Benítez refused to congratulate Sir Alex. 'I prefer to say congratulations to Manchester United; good club, big club.'

When pressed further, he would congratulate them only, and he was quite clear about this, because 'they have won' – and not for *any* other reason than that. But, the bearded Spaniard added, the table doesn't tell you every-thing. The table said Man U had accrued more points than Liverpool. But that wasn't the whole story. 'It just means United have more points.'

He explained: 'If United have more points, it only means they have more points, that's all, nothing else.'

So maybe – maybe – he seemed to hint, Liverpool had won after all? They hadn't. But they might have. If not on points, then surely on . . . don't know.

Asked whether he would be tidying his room later, Benítez answered: 'No chance.'

Financial terms

With the banking crisis, the culture changed quickly and dramatically. Suddenly we became the sort of people who stand round water coolers or smoking outside pubs dis-cussing all kinds of things once deemed boring beyond belief: interest rates, securitisation, whether Britain should have left the Gold Standard in 1931 ('. . . we should never have gone *in*!').

CDOs, HBOS, ISAs . . . Anyone can see how the bankers got into trouble, with all that jargon. Ban acronyms – that would seem to be the lesson here. Luckily, for anyone who feels out of their depth in this new world, here is our ready guide to some of the key phrases that have now entered the lexicon.

Asset Protection Scheme. A scheme. For protecting assets, presumably.

Dead cat bounce. A short-lived upturn in the bounce of a dead cat dropped from a high building. The name derives from the short-lived upturn in the bounce of a dead cat dropped from a high building.

Derivative. A financial instrument without an original bone in its body.

Bear market. Very noisy, angry, rattled market place. On account of all the bears. Agh! The bears are coming! The bears are coming!

CDS. Increasingly superseded by MP3s. Fairly soon, you will be able to show a young person a CDS and they will not know what it's even for.

CDO. Collaterised Debt Obligations – a.k.a., lots of CDSs (credit default swaps) all mixed up together like a shuffled pack of cards, and sold on. Like putting all your CDSs on iTunes, then pressing shuffle. Sadly, the shit : gold ratio often proves surprisingly high. Not more Scissor Sisters already? (i.e. Oh no! Not more defaults in the US mortgage market already?)

Structural investment vehicles. Transportation for getting your money from A to somewhere offshore.

Mezzanine finance. Specialist, high-risk finance that is neither equity nor debt, but which is conducted on a sort of semi-floor, halfway between two proper floors, up some stairs, but not that many stairs. Often there's a café.

L-shaped recovery. Long-lasting. Lean. Lacklustre. Low. Laggardly. Lost. Lonely. Lame. Lamentable. Just some of the 'L' words that ably describe this kind of recovery. I *hate* this sort of recovery.

Platypus bottom. Coined by (the superbly named) UBS trader Art Cashin as a gnomic way of saying, 'I have absolutely no idea what is happening.' As in: 'It lays eggs but it's got webbed feet and spends a lot of time underwater: it's fucked up.'

Stagflation. The rising cost of attending stag events.

Short-selling. A form of market jiggery-pokery often indulged in by hedge funds that involves betting on a decline in the price of shorts. For example, in the autumn.

Naked short-selling. A version of short-selling, illegal or restricted in some jurisdictions, in which the traders sell their own shorts rather than borrowing the shorts from pension funds.

Shadow banking system. Banks taking their activities off-shore and off-balance sheet. It doesn't sound that good, this one, does it? 'I'm in shadow banking.' 'Isn't that, you know, a bit shady?' 'Oh no, not at all. Well, yeah, a bit.'

Zombie banks. Self-explanatory. Deposit cash, jewels, arms, eyes – stuff like that. Open at night. This doesn't sound that healthy, either. What with being named after the living dead.

Synthetic mezzanine CLO squareds. Errrrr . . . don't know. But then, neither does anyone else. The only thing you need to know is that in a rising market, there's always someone who will buy them off you for more than you paid for them. That, by the way, is the secret to the whole world.

Toxic debt. Its build-up caused problems. No shit. It's called toxic debt, for fuck's sake – how obvious could it be that it's bad? What do they want, a smack over the head? (Yes they do.)

Financial Times **'future of capitalism' debate, The**
This series raged in the *FT* for weeks. And they weren't joking either. Every tenet was up for grabs, no holds were

barred. The articles had titles like 'A failure to control animal spirits' and 'Seeds of its own destruction' – phrases traditionally more associated with the millenarian wings of the hard left. They even ran the series in spring. Because this was the new dawn. Rip it up and start again! That was the message here.

Because down at the *FT*, they'd had it with all those snake-oil-selling finance capitalist bastards. Bastards! They were only days away from smashing up their offices and selling their all-new pink paper of justice on the streets. ('Down with the bosses!' 'Yeah, down with them.' 'But aren't we the bosses?' 'Naah . . . well, yeah . . .')

They didn't seem to want to question capitalism much before it all went tits up. But now they definitely, passionately wanted to debate the ethics of the whole thing, the dishonesty, the sham, the sheer gullibility . . . now. Not at the time. Now. Back then, they were probably too busy banking the cheques. But NOW they want to weed out the seeds of destruction. After they've sprouted all over the shop, wreaking, er, destruction.

When capitalism didn't collapse, they swiftly went back into their box, pretending the whole 'Future of Capitalism' rethink never happened. The questioning orgy was over. Red faces all round!

The financial newshounds sheepishly returned to putting their cover price up all the time and increasing the font size so they can use fewer words. All in a desperate bid to keep their particular capitalist ship above the choppy waters. They even held their summer party on the roof of the office, to save money.

Wonder what they talked about? Markets, I expect.

Megan Fox

This Hollywood starlet is the new thing. As in: you might not know her name, but you've seen her tits in the paper.

Always, but always, in every picture of her she has erect nipples. (Seriously, how do people even do that?) And she's always talking about being sexy, loving sex, not minding people thinking she's sexy. I! Literally! Am! Sex! I've got my sexy shoes on, and I'm thinking about sex.

Nothing froths up Internet geeks and the tabloids like a sexy lady talking about sex. They really love that stuff. It makes them froth up like a particularly frisky latte that has been thinking about sex. According to the *Sun*, she looks good even when she's dressed as a nun: 'Sexy Megan is nun the wiser . . . You know someone is of real beauty when they can look hot in a nun's outfit.' Oh yeah. We all know that.

And she's also sexy when covered in blood. Or so reckons, er, the *Sun* (again), accompanying a pointy-nipples picture of the young actress with her white dress caked in blood with the caption: 'Even soaked in blood, Fox proves why she was voted Sexiest Woman in the World. Just quite how Megan Fox remains to look hot while soaked in blood is anyone's guess.' (Fucking hell, that's really dark – even for the *Sun*, that's dark).

So she's great-looking soaked in blood. This much we know. Who knows, maybe she'd even look good covered in gore? But that's not to say she doesn't have a serious side. Particularly when she complained about the *Transformers* films being too reliant on special effects rather than acting.

Director Michael Bay retorted: 'She still has a lot of growing up to do.'

This from a man who makes films about toys fighting each other. And who only cast her in the role after filming her cleaning his Ferrari. And then claiming he'd lost the footage.

In his defence, the director said he thought it was bob-a-job week.

Franco having only one ball

In 2009 it finally emerged that, just like fellow celebrated fascist Adolf Hitler, Spanish dictator General Franco had only one testicle, not the usual complement of two.

At the time of writing, the whereabouts of the other one had yet to be determined. But we know where the smart money is.

Fray Bentos revival, The

'Can you recall the smell when you walked into your grandparents' house on a Sunday lunchtime?' ask articles proclaiming the nation's new (comfort) eating habits.

Old school. Homely mush with lumps in. Just like Granny used to make. Not being able to see across the kitchen for all the steam. Cooking the veg well past the point where it becomes indistinguishable from the boiling water. Then making the gravy with the water from the veg, because 'that's where the goodness is'. (Of course that's where the goodness is, that's where the fucking food is.)

In straitened times, nostalgic comfort food is having a renaissance. People are looking into the salad drawer, rustling through the pink leaves, and saying 'balls to that'. Instead they are reaching into the back of the cupboard for the Bird's Custard Powder and mushy peas – although not hopefully at the same time. Ah yes, those tins: great for an apocalypse *and* a recession.

There are limits, though. Mushy peas in times of stress – that's understandable. But sales of Fray Bentos pies have been going through the roof too. People fleeing to the warm embrace of the tinned pie? I didn't see that one coming. That's pretty much the end of your New Britain right there.

How does eating bad shit count as comforting? Or was Granny big on crap-meat tinned pies too?

You see, that's the great thing about Gran's cooking – nothing ever goes to waste. Always using every last bit of the animal. There she goes, getting her plastic boots on and flaying the carcass with the industrial hose. Waste not, want not!

Friends of the Gurkhas all of a sudden

Gotta love those Gurkhas. Everyone digs the little warrior guys with the bendy weapons. These are wannabe immigrants even the *Daily Mail* can enjoy. Sort of 'our boys', but not. Prince Harry trained with them in the Brecon Beacons and found there were no braver comrades to have alongside you, in the Brecon Beacons.

The Gurkhas' champion is, of course, the great Joanna Lumley. Dame Lumley soon, I should hope: Lady Lumley of Yumley. What a lovely, lovely lady. And still a fox. That's the general line here.

Worked on Gordon Brown, too. The Prime Minister asked her to come and meet him at Number 10. It would only be natural if a little part of him thought: Hmm, I'm going to meet Joanna Lumley here. Okay, we'll be talking about Gurkhas, but still . . . should I stand this side of the desk? Or this side, maybe holding a book? Maybe *my* book? Or is that too much?'

Whatever went on in there, Lumley emerged from Number 10 apparently satisfied. John Pienaar popped up on *PM* claiming that in saying she trusted Brown to do the right thing, she was skilfully 'tying him up with fragrant ropes and scented scarves'. Calm down, Pienaar, you dirty sod. (Wonder if the Gurkhas fancy Joanna Lumley? Does the whole cut-glass posh-totty thing do it for them? Or is it more of a culturally specific thing? *Maybe* that's not the most urgent question here. But still worth knowing the answer.)

The Lumley-powered parliamentary routing of the government was fairly amazing, if surreal. But let's not be too swayed by rampant Lumleyism here: it has been brought to my attention that a significant minority of Gurkhas actually prefer Diana Rigg. 'I am preferring Diana Rigg,' said my source on this, repeating words he claimed another source had said to him. 'The original *Avengers* is much better – not just sexy, storylines too.'

In the interest of fairness, I should point out that other Gurkhas, from the Gurkha majority, often retort: 'Look at the whole career, though. Not just *Avengers*, not just Patsy. Also the prostitute in *Shirley Valentine*. "I'm not an air hostess darling, I'm a high-class hooker."'

To which the original Gurkha says: '*Mad Cows* – load of shit!' And so it goes on.

I say everyone loves the Gurkhas, but actually, a week before the vote I didn't once come across anyone all that vexed about the Gurkhas. People didn't generally respond to the question 'So, what have you been up to?' with 'I've been writing letters to my MP about the Gurkhas again. It's a full-time job with me, the Gurkhas.' That didn't happen.

So it's fine everyone getting into the Gurkhas once they're fashionable, but what about the real fans? Now, all of a sudden, the right-wing press is splashing with 'Ayo Gurkhali' – basically, in this case meaning, 'A load of foreign immigrants are coming!' Only this time being really jubilant about it.

Still, it's cool the *Mail* now wants to let in people who've 'done something for Britain'. If that includes being colonised by, being economically drained by or being otherwise invaded by Britain, isn't that pretty much everyone? That's quite a leap there: from no one, to everyone.

Let's hope the Gurkhas don't set things back by claiming benefits, knocking up teenagers, stealing jobs or somehow driving down house prices.

Maybe they're planning on setting up some truly horrendous sound systems. They seem like pretty quiet guys now . . .

FSA pledging to get scary

The Financial Services Authority is on the warpath. Lock up your daughters. And shred any incriminating accounting documents. Probably do that before locking up your daughters.

When new chief executive Hector Sants said people 'should be very frightened' of the FSA, he sent shivers around the nation. Except the City. The bankers couldn't give a fuck. Because, really, if the FSA stood by as you wreaked the biggest banking havoc the world has ever known, so much so that you even put the shits up yourself, well . . . what's the worst that's going to happen here? What have you actually got to do to ring alarm bells with this lot anyway? Strangle people by the window of your office, with the lights on, at rush hour? Maybe hanging them out of the window while strangling them? Would they even notice?

Really it's hard to get excited about an investigator who knows about things only after everyone else. I know about shoddy bank practices. I saw it on the news. That doesn't make me a regulatory authority, though. Not in and of itself.

FSA AGENT: Boss, I've found some serious banking irregularities we need to be looking into.
FSA BOSS: Been working your contacts?
FSA AGENT: No, I saw it on the news. Sounded appalling.

There was an opening for bringing down hellfire on Mammon. They missed it.

G

Gardening on the moon

There's quite a gardening thing going on these days, with all the allotments and that. And best of luck to them, provided they do it quietly and stop writing books or talking about it. Even Michelle Obama's at it and, as we know, she's hot!

But you have to doubt, in a world of scarce resources, with cutting stuff back definitely in vogue, on the efficacy of launching gardeners into space. It's not like there are any gardens there, for starters.

Sidestepping these minor concerns, Paragon Space Development has unveiled plans to land mini-greenhouses on the fucking moon to see if they can grow Brussels sprouts (I'm not making this up) on the fucking moon.

It's only slightly less pointless than North Korea, a country that can't even feed people enough rice, firing off rockets to piss off Obama. (They did actually piss off Obama, though, so job done their end, I suppose.)

'Colonising the Moon or Mars seems so far away [no shit],' said Paragon president Jane Poynter, launching the plan to grow vegetables from the brassica family, including sprouts and cabbage, 'but it is important that we do this research now.'

Personally, I never thought I'd live to see the day. The day we put a Brussels sprout on the moon. I did dream, but no more than that. Wonder how the first Brussels sprout on the moon will readjust to normal life, though.

A boozy, culty Brussels sprout – that's something we *don't* need.

Gay exorcisms

At first, I thought this sounded quite a laugh. Like your normal exorcism – repealing demons from the souls of the possessed – only more gay. Not necessarily gay in a stereo-typical, gays-on-telly way – arms flapping everywhere and jokes about the laying on of hands. Just less relentlessly heterosexual than your average exorcism. We've all had enough of that dated shit.

Then I realised it was about African-Christian churches in London exorcising the gayness out of people. Which doesn't sound very gay at all. The Reverend John Ogbe-Ogbeide of the United Pentecostal Ministry in Harrow holds four or five exorcisms a year and claims they always work.

I'm not convinced. Footage of an American ritual showed a vulnerable sixteen-year-old boy being thrown onto the floor to be stood on and yelled at by crazies for twenty minutes, before, traumatised, vomiting into a bag – I can see how this might make him not feel massively like having sex at all, but . . . Child Abuse for Jesus they could call it.

Still, at least these über-Christian freaks aren't standing in elections. Oh no, hang on . . .

Malcolm Gladwell

Malcolm Gladwell was recently acclaimed as the 'most influential thinker in the world'. This self-professed 'intellectual adventurer' had already wowed the reading public with bestselling books like *The Tipping Point*, which pointed out how sometimes things reach a tipping point, and *Blink*, about how ideas often just come to people just like that (or do they?), and *Outliers*, which pointed out that successful people often need to work hard to make the most of themselves.

Then came the event that will come to define his career. Gladwell had easily filled out the Albert Hall with paying admirers keen to hear him expound on his new thesis Some You Win, Some You Lose. But as the age's premier conceptual lightning rod took to the stage, the muse struck *again*:

'Okay, I'm throwing out my notes. I'll warn you now: this could be the big one. With my surprising new concept, I shall aim to answer the question of how some things can be so overrated that it's actually weird. This is the new concept which I think I will call "Weirdly Overrated".

'If I may dip into my own personal story here for a second – forgive my indulgence! – I now believe my own works are the very essence of "Weirdly Overrated". As of this moment, even I cannot see what anyone sees in my books – and they're my books!

'But I think I can extrapolate even further: could it be that, if I am Weirdly Overrated, then everything else is Weirdly Overrated too? Is the Weirdly Overrated phenomenon fanning out from my books to encompass everything else too? Is it *all* my fault? Or is it the world's fault? I actually think it's a little bit of both . . .

'Anyway, gotta go now. Better write all this down before I forget it. Put some stats in – something about, hmmm, let's see . . . Steve Jobs, rice-cakes, Michael Jordan, Aerosmith, rock-climbing, fried chicken, John Dos Passos, Bertolucci, cream cheese, the Count of Monte Cristo . . . Etc.'

And the Albert Hall was rocked to its rafters as the people cheered and cheered and stamped their feet. Hooray! Hooray for Malcolm Gladwell! Hooray! It's his best yet! Hooray!

And Malcolm Gladwell merely raised an eyebrow in a quizzical manner.

Going-without articles

'I gave up wheat for a year.'

'I gave up barley for a year.'

'I gave up meat for a year.'

'I gave up sex for a year.'

'I gave up meat-sex for a year.'

'I dressed as a man for a year.'

'I was the witch of Wookey Hole for a year.'

'I had sex every day for a year – which is going without not having sex.'

'I didn't sleep for a week!'

'I didn't eat for a week!'

'I gave up e-mails.'

'I gave up she-males.'

'I gave up nails.'

'I gave up No More Nails – I had planned on keeping this up for a year, but I barely even lasted the week! Don't put me through *that* again . . . Nails? Brrr.'

Fred Goodwin looking for another job in banking

At one point at the start of 2009, tabloid editors were less interested in paparazzi pics of Britney Spears than pics of Fred Goodwin enjoying himself. It didn't matter what he was doing – tobogganing, judo or reading a comic – just as long as he was enjoying himself, that would be enough.

Given the sudden interest in his private affairs, the former RBS boss unsurprisingly went into hiding. In the South of France.

But that was months ago. Now he's done his time. Not inside. Mainly outside. And he's 'done the right thing' – finally agreeing voluntarily to reduce his annual reward for failure to £342,500 a year. And now he's back. And he knows what he wants.

It's just another little job in banking, please.

According to an industry source in July 2009, Fred Goodwin is sick of being a pariah and wants to get home, 'possibly with a view to working in the banking sector again'. Apparently, there's only so much time you can spend sitting around in the French sunshine, and so 'Fred believes that a concession in his pension benefits will win back public confidence. He feels he's been punished enough and wants to hold his head up high back in Britain.'

Fred Goodwin is happy to give things another go if you are. You've called him some nasty names. You've broken his windows. You've really put him through it. He even lost his job over the whole thing. All just for that one time – it was only the once! – that he helped break the national purse and crash the world economy.

But he's been working some things out and now he thinks it's time to try again. There's so much history there, it would be a shame just to let it all go.

Can't you see? He needs this. The man is crying out here. He hasn't fucked anyone up in months.

Green shoots

First it was wrong to see green shoots. Then it was okay to see green shoots. Then it was not okay to see green shoots but it was okay to see green seedlings. Then they said that just because you couldn't see green shoots, that didn't mean they didn't exist. Can't see any green shoots? Well, that may be a sure sign of green shoots. Then we were warned not to mistake sunny weather for green shoots. Yes, some people out there are *still* mistaking sunny weather for green shoots. Arseholes.

So there's been a lot of stuff about green shoots. Essentially, what was being forecast here was pretty much a pure and simple stock market revival ... because they believe that things will get better in the real world in a year, or eighteen months, or two years, or beyond. So what we're supposed to be getting excited about is some specu-lators starting to make money again. While everything is still unravelling (houses, jobs, etc.) for everyone else. So one paper's headline might be 'Signs of recovery', while another on the same day will be 'Massive youth unemployment'.

So, basically, you can stick your green shoots right up your arse.

G20, The

In April 2009, with the world economy in perilous chaos, world leaders met in London for a chat. This historic meeting, the G20, was so-called because there were twenty-four countries represented, suggesting that the inaccurate and, some would say, corrupt maths that had created the problems was not exactly being tackled root and branch.

This was a gathering of paramount importance. Some would even say of world historical importance. And the key question of the day was clear: Michelle Obama – is she hot, or what? (Michelle Obama herself modestly claimed that she is not hot. Even though she is.) And also one other big question: exactly how hot?

God, the pair of them! They're so freakin' hot! They're the most powerful couple on the planet; bet you wouldn't mind being the meat in that sandwich, would you? Hot! Hot! Hot! That is what some people were saying at the time, anyway.

Hot! Where was I? Oh yeah, G20, stimulus, economics,

blah blah (hot!). Here is what happened. As with all the best training days, the G20 Panic Stations of Nations Day started at 10–10.30 a.m. with Arrival and Registration. Refreshments were provided by Jamie Oliver who, having promised honest catering with no 'fancy ingredients', laid on a quintessential British welcome of individual packets of biscuits plus lukewarm tea in extremely small polystyrene cups. (Oliver was seen going round to anyone who would listen – Mariella Frostrup, Dmitry Medvedev – bigging up the Great British Lunch he was preparing: 'Flan, barbecue wings, you name it . . . I've been up marge-ing sarnies since half past six this morning, mate.')

There was a bit of a to-do because the Americans were late. This created problems for the media, which had become the can-barely-contain-itself conduit for worldwide expectation, veering erratically between 'feverish' and 'quivering'. Sophie Raworth had already had to be sent home after she started revolving on the *BBC Breakfast* sofa, freaking out kids who were watching. There was a definite risk, said a conveyor belt of commentators, of governments doing too little. Equally, there was a risk of them doing too much. Or the wrong things. Or a mixture of all those. Anything could happen. That's what the experts were predicting.

Everyone thought the Americans were being deliberately late to look cool. But they had an entourage of five hundred (not including embassy staff already here) so it just took ages to organise a crocodile down to the Tube. Five hundred American tourists trying to get their heads round the new prepay Oyster cards? Carnage.

At the conference centre, journalists, high on caffeine

and very sweaty, were by now a roaming pack of animals looking for titbits and free soup, cornering world leaders and demanding to know: 'Have you got Michelle Obama's mobile number? Give me Michelle Obama's mobile number. Fucking give it to me!' In a desperate bid to break the tension, Chinese President Hu Jintao made a joke about starting without the Americans, but it fell flat. 'Look, it was a fucking joke,' he protested. 'An ice-breaker. And I don't mean Alaskan ice, as the Glorious People's Republic passes through to invade. Oh, come on! Lighten up already.'

The Americans are here! The Americans are here! Turns out they got on the wrong connection at Baker Street. *Now* it's game on. *This* is what we're talking about.

It's lunch! As Oliver pours various flavours of Hula Hoops into bowls, Obama breaks off for a cheeky side meeting of the truly powerful, the so-called G2: this is where the President of the United States sits down, breaks bread and talks turkey with the people who do the tabloid section of the *Guardian*, the lifestyle features and that. After sending out for more of Jamie's Marmite sandwiches with the crusts cut off, Obama also meets with China, then Russia, then China *and* Russia, then Russia *and* China (the latter so neither gets pissed off by theirs not being the first name listed). Arms are discussed. The USA and Russia say they want lots. China says they also want some, and everyone says that's cool.

On Threadneedle Street, in the City, a window is broken. Somewhere in Japan, a butterfly flaps its wings and four thousand Greek people lose their jobs.

Business time. It is business time. But first a presentation

BARROSO: I'll write that down. Oh, hang on: how many zeros are there?

OBAMA: I'll get my people on to that.

OBAMA SENDS SOME PEOPLE OFF TO GET A FIGURE FOR HOW MANY ZEROES THERE ARE IN A TRILLION. ALL THE OTHER WORLD LEADERS WISH THEY WERE THAT COOL AND HAD PEOPLE TO FIND OUT ABOUT NUMBERS FOR THEM.

OBAMA: Not knowing how many zeros there are is *exactly* the sort of thing that would make us look stupid in front of the press.

MERKEL: It's a lot of money to find.

OBAMA: Can't be that much. We can include all the money we've already committed.

SARKOZY: And then not front up all the rest of it. Just pretend we're going to.

BERLUSCONI: Yeah, but still claim the tax back on it. Er, did I say that out loud?

AS THEY START TO FILE OUR, GORDON BROWN REMEMBERS SOMETHING.

BROWN: Hang on! What about toxic activity. Shouldn't we legislate against toxic activity?

OBAMA: Maybe. What's the point, though? Everyone knows toxic is bad. It's all there in the name. It'd be like passing a law stopping people eating tarmac.

MERKEL: Tax havens?

OBAMA: Keep it vague.

BROWN: Regulation?

OBAMA: Keep it vague.

BROWN: All those in favour of keeping everything vague say 'aye'.

THE LEADERS OF THE WORLD: Aye!

AS THEY START TO FILE OUT, GORDON BROWN REMEMBERS SOMETHING.

BROWN: What about the environment?

BERLUSCONI: Fuck the environment. Let's spend!

[General laughter.]

BROWN: But I've promised a global Green New Deal.

OBAMA: It's okay, Brian, no one remembers anything you say.

HU JINTAO: Hey, this lending to low-income economies bullshit? We could reparcel the debt and sell it on at a profit. Joke! It was . . . it was a joke. Great, so now Obama's looking at me like I'm some sort of twat.

OBAMA: It's okay. We're cool.

HU JINTAO: Yeah, as long as we keep lending you money we're cool. Joke! Another joke.

BROWN: Agreed then. We go and get our photo taken with the Queen – except Obama, where the Queen will have her photo taken with him, obviously – and look like we know what we're doing. A trillion pounds! No – dollars! A trillion dollars. I knew that.

In the evening, while the world's leaders enjoy Oliver's dinner of 'honest high-street products' (Sausage au Beans à la Aunt Bessie), Sarah Brown holds a party for 'the wives', at which they buy Tupperware from each other. A small disabled child is brought in and they ceremonially hug the child. Then they dance and they dance and they dance, until the whole damn mess disappears in a twirl of Michelle Obama's skirt.

And, you know, they never did find out how many zeros make a trillion. But by then it didn't really matter. Everyone was pretending everything was all right again. Which, in a way, it was.

And yet, in other ways, it wasn't.

Sshhh. Don't mention the environment.

G20 protest tourists

Demonstrators 'kettled' outside the Bank of England by police, not allowed to leave, busting for a wee, should have at least been able to console themselves that it was the one place on earth they could be guaranteed not to run into A.A. Gill. But no, he denied us even that small pleasure.

Old A.A. was down the front (where else?), having his face painted green by a Climate Camp activist/'pretty girl' called Paris, and generally recording for posterity the 'hot totty', 'snogging', 'pretty eco-warriors' and, of course, the 'nubile girls'. God, he loved the girls.

You can't go on a demonstration these days without tripping over broadsheet features writers 'feeling it'. It's like in the 90s when Glastonbury was suddenly adopted as part of the media calendar, and every media outlet had to cover it religiously . . . the *Guardian* started sending a *G2* bus down (an actual, er, bus), and *Mail* writers would disappear into the Green Field for days, with some even rumoured to have blown their minds on 'shrooms and gravitated up the Tor to perform a decade-long living play about Avalon, the mystical land of the past which is also inside us all.

Now it's protests. So the Financial Fools Day demo had Gill and an assorted crew of demo-liggers including the deputy editor of *Vogue*, Emily Sheffield, and, for the *Telegraph*, Celia Walden – who usually writes articles called things like 'Yes, Cannes is frivolous and absurd, but I still love it!' ('Yet despite – or maybe because of – the recession, the parties were sublime . . .') Walden was clutching an 'embarrassingly pristine' placard proclaiming: 'The *Daily Telegraph* wants: Lower taxes now! Free trade now! Roll back the state!'

How everyone laughed. They thought it was ironic! But it wasn't! 'Yet despite – or maybe because of – being kettled in by riot police, the demo was sublime . . . frivolous and absurd, yes, but glorious! I mean, like, what is the system, yeah?'

No wonder the media were all over the protests, though. The police had promised 'innovative' demo tactics, to include rabid anarchists 'launch[ing] inflatable dinghies in an attempt to breach the summit security at the Excel centre in Docklands via the river Thames'.

After they'd so spectacularly breached the sea defences, presumably these 'anarchist groups' would send in their Apache helicopter gunships and advance ground forces? This was the fear at the Yard. And who wouldn't want to see that?

In the event, the demonstrators' innovations mainly involved marching, waving banners and chanting. There were some papier mâché Horsemen of the Apocalypse: quite innovative possibly, but not much use for seabound attacks on the world's elite security forces. Not unless they were the real Four Horsemen of the Apocalypse. Which they weren't.

For their part, the police eschewed new-fangled ways for old-school techniques, like hitting people with sticks.

H

Haggle bores

Getting the things you need for the cheapest price seems a sensible course of action generally. But then people start getting obsessed with it, talking you through blow-by-blow exchanges with some bloke in Comet in real time, forgetting that the entirety of their exciting tale boils down to: I have purchased a new vacuum cleaner.

Some people take it even further. In recessionary times, these so-called 'dark hagglers' feel more able to discuss their crazed obsessions in polite company. Watch out for anyone discussing the art of charity-shop haggling: 'It's just old bids. Easy meat.'

Nonetheless, you should not resist the urge for the occasional haggle – moderately engaged in, with a polite air. Here is everything you need to know for successful haggling, as detailed by Dom Littlewood of BBC's *To Buy or Not to Buy* in a dream I had recently after one too many Mint Imperials:

- Look the shop assistant in the eye, grabbing their arm firmly. Ask: 'What's the best you can do on this?' As they answer – that is, while they are answering – shout in their face: 'Are you having a fucking laugh?'

- No one ever fails in negotiations by going in either too high or too low. Split your options here. First offer them twice the ticket price, then – laughing – say: 'Actually, I'll give you a quid. What do you say? You've got till Sunday.' Remember to look them in the eye and grab them by the arm. Once you've made your offer, say absolutely nothing at all – make him sweat. Don't even speak if he agrees to your price, asks you to leave, anything like that. Own that mother.
- It pays to establish a rapport. Eye contact and arm holding are good here, but also find out the assistant's name. Then look him up on Facebook, and pretend you know his dad. Say things like: 'Do you ever see Tony any more? I do and he's dead from cancer – knock a tenner off that food-mixer, it's what he would have wanted.'
- Always keep in mind your ideal price for the product. Then throw this sum over the counter while running out of the store with the goods. Yes, alarms may sound: it doesn't matter; you have haggled successfully and got what you wanted.
- Taxi drivers in particular *love* haggling. So do publicans.

Tom Hanks being at the 2009 D-Day memorial in Normandy

All the old units were reunited to commemorate their lost comrades in arms: 2 Para, 1st Canadian Para, US 17th Airborne ... and the guy from *Saving Private Ryan*.

Because, in a way, Tom Hanks lived it too. Well, he pretended to, anyway. And he was, to be fair, bloody convincing.

All the vets love to see him there. Yes, this is partly because he's a film star. But it's also more than that: he's the most famous man to have actually been there – on the set of *Saving Private Ryan*. We should make the most of him while he's still here.

Matt Damon didn't have the basic fucking decency to turn up, I notice. Nor did Tom Sizemore (what *possibly* could have been keeping Sizemore?). But Hanks, yes. He also pitched up in 2001 for the fifty-seventh anniversary of D-Day, using the event to publicise the *Band of Brothers* TV series. Commemorating the dead on the beaches in Normandy because he was once in a film about it – that's his thing.

He's always over there. You have to ask: is Tom Hanks gradually trying to invade France? He might be. He is quite unpredictable.

Still, he did fuck a mermaid. And not many people can say that. Not these days.

Having to read the business pages

Before now, the very definition of 'a fag', but once they started trying to punch human society to its knees, you think: Well, I'll just have a *little* look.

These are, for now, your actual news pages – where the shit happens. You can find out some pretty amazing stuff there, it turns out – how all the oil companies are binning renewables, how speculators boosting the price of rice is causing food riots . . . Nothing good. You don't tend to find out anything good there, not generally. But you do find out *stuff*. Often quite important stuff.

One day you might open the BBC website's Business News page to be confronted with: 'Barclays boss attacks bank lending "lunacy"' . . . (God, bankers, eh? Bloody loonies . . . Not me, though!)

Plus: 'Reckless bosses "must be stopped" . . . a Treasury minister says.' (That is, the people who were supposed to stop them say they must be stopped.)

Plus: 'ALSO IN THE NEWS . . . Mexico's most wanted man makes it on to the *Forbes* Rich List.' (So he's wanted in so many ways.)

You have to wonder: was it always like this? All those years of blissfully reading the news-news – or 'the main news', as it's sometimes called – and then turning to the racing . . . was there always a world of crisis and turmoil and misdeed hiding out back there, in the bits no one reads?

Yeah, well I'm on to you. Like many other people, I am now a reader of the business pages. Not every day. Not even alternate days. But some days.

Definitely most Sundays, and sometimes weekdays too.

So watch out – that's all I'm saying.

Her Majesty's action men

Action Man! He's back. And this time, he's genuinely in the army.

The new range of Ministry of Defence-sponsored soldier-dolls even look like the old ones. There's the same 'no willy' groin region, and ruggedly handsome features (well, I used to fancy him anyway). But this time the military toys are actually provided by the military, under the brand 'HM Armed Forces', with profits heading straight into the MoD public relations fund. (The armed forces feel the need to generate some good PR, after all the illegal wars and stuff, and who can say they're not right?)

At the launch, Squadron Leader Stuart Balfour claimed: 'We feel by children playing with these toys, it promotes things like discipline, a sense of belonging to a wider organisation and teamwork.' So, it's all about encouraging children to see the army in a positive way – like a cool club you can join.

So is this up-to-date soldiery getting some modern baddies to fight? After all, kids just aren't as obsessed with German storm-troopers as they used to be. There are plans to bring out a villain, but he will not – that's not – resemble an al-Qaeda terrorist.

'We don't want to get into that,' said toymaker Jon Driver.

Wise words. So instead, the baddie will resemble 'a random mercenary'. This could create confusion, though. What if Action Man hires the random mercenary to carry out illegal acts for him on the sly – you know, like in Iraq? What will that do to the children's sense of discipline and belonging?

Also, they could have given them willies. That's the *least* they could have done.

High-to-let

Landlords are being urged to keep a look-out for tenants setting up cannabis farms. Apparently, one key sign is all the windows being taped over. That's right: as the owner of a property, you are perfectly within your rights to wonder why the tenants have blacked out all the windows.

'Why have they blacked out the windows?' That's what you might ask yourself.

Hitler intending to make Blackpool his personal post-invasion of Britain holiday home, Revelations of

According to documents recently unearthed in Germany, the Luftwaffe largely spared the Lancashire resort from bombing raids, despite the war-related manufacturing near by, for one reason: Hitler wanted to go there on his holidays.

Golden mile? Nazi mile, more like. The whole town was going to be the Fuhrer's post-invasion 'playground', with a swastika flapping atop the Tower as Hitler dipped his toes in the icy waters below, perhaps even enjoying a ninety-*neun*.

Going through material related to Operation Sealion, Michael Cole discovered plans to drop German forces into the Stanley Park 'Italian' gardens (easily visible from the air) before heading into town. 'Time it right for pound a pint night,' ordered the Fuhrer.

There were also numerous German intelligence maps, plus aerial photos of the town and a range of saucy cartoon postcards that would be considered sexist by modern standards. (Hitler was evidently not bothered about charges of sexism.)

The thing is, though – and no disrespect to Blackpool (although anyone who has been there recently might find it hard to believe it wasn't bombed) – you would think that with the whole of the British Isles to choose from, Hitler might have fancied, say, Robin Hood's Bay? Southwold? The Gower Peninsula? Clearly, questioning Hitler's judgement is hardly a bold step, but Blackpool? It hardly reeks of *sturm und drang*. I mean, Scarborough, possibly . . .

Anyway, Göring did suggest Brighton, but the Fuhrer felt there were too many media wankers moving down from London.

Honey rustling

Prince Charles has had his bees rustled. This sounds like it might mean something rude, but it doesn't. This is not about the birds and the bees. It's just about the bees. Which have been nicked.

Bee rustlers have been striking up and down the length of cash-strapped Britain – nicking bees. Hives have become hives of criminal activity, by being stolen. In June 2009 someone even broke into a field in Scotland and stole half a million bees in one go. (How did they know it was half a million? Rounding it up for the insurance, I expect.)

The biggest theft happened at a strawberry farm in Shropshire, where eighteen hives containing about a million bees used to pollinate the strawberry crop were stolen.

Owner Richard Lindsey estimated the haul 'could be worth up to £6000 on the black market'.

The black market? The black market in bees?

Surely when the rustlers go down the pub and say 'Psst, want some bees?' and open up the tatty holdall, all the bees will just fly out and sting innocent drinkers. Black market? Distinctly dissatisfied-going-on-traumatised pub-goer market more like. Bee-infested pub-mare, to be completely accurate about it.

You'd have to be pretty desperate to rustle bees, for obvious reasons. Either that, or be an expert in bees and bee-control. Maybe it's not a crime inspired by economic necessity and they just do it for the buzz? Sorry, sorry, sorry.

Put the bees in the bag and no one gets hurt! Show me the honey! That's the sort of thing you could shout.

Apparently, someone also stole some cows off the Queen. Don't know if it's connected. It's all getting a bit like that bit in the Ken Loach film *Raining Stones*, where Jim Royle and Les Battersby try to steal a sheep . . . only not a film.

Anyway, bees have it tough enough already, with populations declining rapidly for little-understood reasons and threatening various ecosystems. So leave the bees alone, people. Stop nicking the bees. You fucking mentalists.

Horne and Corden

Hopefully, future cultural historians will pinpoint this show as the nadir. If not, if there is something coming worse than this, then truly we are fucked.

At the moment, I'm still holding on to the idea that Horne and Corden were either trying to pre-empt the backlash or were sick of all the adulation and wanted to get people off their cases.

Although it doesn't look like they're *very* sick of all the adulation.

Houses that Saved the World, The

If you are on the lookout for the best economists, one place to look is *The Economist*: it's what *The Economist* is all about. Well, that and adverts for watches. Having said that, *The Economist*'s take on America's sub-prime housing market was summed up in the 2002 front-cover headline, 'The Houses that Saved the World'.

So that's wrong. Okay, you can sort of see where they were coming from. It was the early twenty-first century. Recent wheezes – deregulated energy and the Internet – had gone to cock in a blaze of hubris and fraud (now *that's* writing about economics) leaving an urgent need to get that wealth working again. Capital needed 'stuff' to invest in. In short, there was a hole where a bubble should be.

But here was a bubble that would never blow up – what's as safe as houses? It's even a ruddy phrase! So they lent vast wodges to people with hardly any money and little prospect of getting any. Cities like Detroit were suddenly plagued by a new infestation of predatory lenders. Yes, we know this sounds like the Western elites literally turning themselves into sink-estate loan sharks, but it's really not like that. If it was like that, this would certainly be quite a damning final defining image for the Reaganomic dream. But it wasn't. For a start, they didn't break people's legs. They just took away their homes.

Still, *The Economist* considering all this as 'saving the world': isn't this the kind of sunny outlook we could do with more of in this day and age?

I

Ideological subtext of late-period *Bob the Builder*

Times of crisis lay bare the workings of power, and shine a light of truth even into the recesses of children's television. The political superstructure of Bob the so-called Builder, for example, becomes obvious to even the most naive of tots. And it's some powerful shit.

The various machines in Bob's yard – Lofty, Dizzy, Scrambler *et al.* – are a 'team'. 'Working together' they not only 'get the job done' but 'have fun'. Yes: work is fun. That is the mythos of Bob.

But, once they have collectively cleaned out Mrs Potts' guttering, who from this 'team' keeps all the profits? Or, should we say, appropriates the surplus value? Yes, that's Bob, a.k.a. The Man.

The worker-machines – Muck, Roley, Scoop *et al.* – are alive, they speak, but they answer only to Bob. He *possesses* them. And where does this animated exploiter live? Bobsville. Like some bewhiskered Victorian business baron, Bob has styled the town in his own image.

In one episode, Scoop looks up builders in the phone-book: only Bob is listed – the natural consequence of all so-called 'free' markets, the monopoly. The worker-machines resort to getting in Bob's dad: also a builder, also called Bob. 'Once a builder,' says Bob's dad, 'always a builder.' The message is plain: get rid of one so-called Bob the Builder and there will *always* be another. This is the natural order. Resistance is futile.

Bob's shadowy presence as the four-fingered hand in all Bobsville's pies is underlined when Bernard Bentley becomes Mayor. Bernard's former job? Building inspector. Say no more on that fucking score. (What happened to the old Mayor? Propping up the foundations of those newbuild flats Bob knocked up over by the station, I expect.)

And what of Bob's will-they-won't-they relationship with Wendy? The simmering sexual tension bursts from the screen causing, daily, parents across the land silently to scream: 'Oh, for fuck's sake, man, just give her one!' (Usually silently.) Here Bob shows the limits of his own existence: unable to relate to his workforce on equal terms, he hides behind his power, building the object of his affections an absurd Xanadu – a solar-powered caravan home in Sunflower Valley. (Wendy can't afford a proper house, not on the wages Bob the Bastard's paying her.)

Finally, there is Spud (ah, Spud), the ragged-trousered scarecrow with a carrot for a nose. Like a latter-day Lord of Misrule, Spud is forever slacking off and transgressing boundaries, his drug-eyes flashing and bulging. Whatever they say he is, that's what he's not. But Spud always ends up in an unholy mess: getting stuck up a tree, or falling off a bridge. And who bails him out every time? Yes, it's Bob the Godhead, the Unmoveable Force. Don't stray outside the system, kids, for that way chaos lies. To question the norms of Sunflower Valley is to fail. You will get stuck up a tree, metaphorically and sometimes literally.

Can he 'fix' it? It certainly fucking looks like it.

'I don't think it'll effect property prices around here', The phrase

That's right. Because *you* are very, very special.

Irish economic miracle, The

The cranes! Oh, the cranes. The craning cranes. For years, no one left Dublin without a stiff neck from looking up at all the cranes. People came from all over Europe, just to see the cranes. Dublin's skyline was changed, changed utterly – by cranes. What were the cranes building? Blocks of 'luxury apartments'. And who would live in them? Er . . . don't know . . . some people?

Ireland's economy was an example of low-tax, low-regulation genius – third only to Hong Kong and Singapore as the world's most free market economy. In the high times, the bankers kept lending money to their friends, the builders (a powerful property clique dubbed, literally, The Builders); money which they had in turn borrowed at low rates from the EU. Add in high-level corruption scandals (Taoiseach Bertie Ahern resigned in 2008 over allegations of payments from, er, property developers) and you have to ask: what could possibly go wrong?

The builders were building like there was no tomorrow,

but there was a tomorrow and, while Dublin was awash with cash, it was still not massively awash with actual people. So, as it transpired, Dublin was changed, changed utterly – by empty apartments blocks. Indeed, all over Ireland, snow would soon be falling, upon all the living and the dead – and the empty apartments blocks.

Isn't this just like Britain? Well, yes, but more so, and bearing down on far fewer people. By April 2009, the property boom economy was in tatters – unemployment, taxes and negative equity were all rising – and Ireland's creditworthiness was dramatically downgraded by ratings agency Moody's (a bummer if Ireland's government ever needs to buy any white goods on tic).

Anyway, who better to inspire the Irish to rise anew, as it surely must, than its wordsmiths? Sadly, many of those left Ireland after tax breaks for writers and artists were repealed. Luckily, we can still turn to Spiral, the Dublin MC, from *Big Brother 7*. Here is Spiral's response to events . . .

Construction
Is corruption
And now even Bono's
Gone and got the hump on

The new taxation
Is vexation
If you're the shortest singer in the nation

Boom! Boom! Yeah!
Went the boom, yeah!

Because they went and built
Far too many rooms, yeah

And the economy
Fell down in front of me
It's the epitome
Of bank chicanery

You just remember me
Leering at Aisleyne
But my words
They are truer than Trueclean

You know that Ireland
It sounds like Iceland
That may be why we're feelin'
Fiscally tightened?

Was it proximity
In the dictionary?
Did I tell you I'm available for parties?

J

Michael Jackson supplements

Wasn't this just sick? After all the supplements that made his poor heart finally go 'Ow!' – the morphine-like supplements, the Valium-like supplements, the painkilling supplements, the muscle-relaxing supplements, the anti-anxiety supplements, the anti-heartburn supplements – for the world's media to respond to his death with loads *more* supplements? These people are such thoughtless bastards, it's not true.

In fairness, these supplements often contained well-balanced tributes to the man's talent, his talent and also his talent. Taking in the songs: I Want You Back (there was a lot about I Want You Back) and also Bad (okay, not Bad, but definitely I Want You Back).

And the dancing: the grabbing of his crotch, and also the tilting his hat. He was good at that. No one could say he couldn't tilt his hat forward and go 'Ooh!' Because he could. (Although you do wonder if he was really happy – even when he was going 'Ooh!')

But I can't help thinking the well-balanced tributes did miss another of his talents: they were COMPLETELY FORGETTING that he was also a culinary innovator – he was the man behind Jesus Juice! That is, white wine served in cans of Diet Coke. Okay, so it's not the classiest way to serve white wine. But it is a great way to get kids pissed.

Why would you want to get kids pissed? Why would anyone want to get *anyone* pissed? For the conversation, of course!

Incidentally, I surely wasn't the only one shocked to see the headline 'Jackson's Kids Left to Ross in Will'. For a second there, I was aghast at the thought of those poor children being left at the mercy of Jonathan Ross. With his foul-mouthed phone calls and lowering of standards. I was livid.

Then I realised they meant Ross Kemp. That's okay, he'll protect them.

Digby Jones: are you still here?

This isn't, strictly speaking, 'Digby's crisis' – this one's even bigger than him (and he is one fat fucker). But then again, it's not *not* 'his crisis' either. The former Confederation of British Industry chief and business tsar ennobled by Gordon Brown was not *not* a fairly unabashed 'let the market decide' kind of guy. And not *not* a 'hideous fucking poster-boy for all the lies we've had to swallow for the past thirty years'.

So, really, of all the people to pop up on Channel 4's *Dispatches* investigating the jobs crisis, bemoaning the effect of the recession on the little man, this big man might – might – just be the worst possible option barring, say, Milton Friedman.

And yet here he is – on my fucking telly – meeting

Richard, a recently unemployed skilled worker: 'Richard was not engaged in a job that was froth. He was engaged as a skilled man. Why did we get into this position?'

Er, flexible labour market? 'Business needs flexible labour market, says CBI' – remember that? Taking people on, laying people off . . . Or by flexible workforce, did you just mean more yoga and that?

Then he puts it to then-minister Tony McNulty that Job Centre Plus is 'not fit for purpose' since the government cut thirty-thousand jobs – despite the fact he ended his short stint in government saying that half of civil servants could easily be sacked. (Unless he thinks job centres are staffed by milkmaids, which he may.)

So it's not *not* 'Digby's crisis'. And the fact he now has the nerve to complain about people being hung out to dry makes him not *not* a total cunt-and-a-half who, if he had any shame left in his soul whatsoever, would find the nearest sandy beach and bury himself in it, with nothing sticking out, just fucking staying there, not even his stupid fucking hair, for ever and fucking ever.

Will he, though? Will he fuck.

Jones on Jones and Cameron in *Cameron on Cameron*

First it was iPods that *GQ* editor Dylan Jones was writing book-length encomiums about. Now, apparently, the stylish man about town should not be seen without a David Cameron. In 2007 *GQ* made Cameron their second-best-dressed man of the year after Daniel Craig . . . God, they love Daniel Craig. (Clive Owen was third, in case you're wondering.)

Then Jones spent a whole year talking to Cameron (with breaks, presumably). The book *Cameron on Cameron* was the result. Needless to say, he liked what he heard, and saw, and probably even smelled – the title itself refers to one of the author's own sexual fantasies . . .

'A sharp-suited firebrand . . . dynamic speeches . . . your self-confidence is blinding . . . a speech that changed the British political landscape . . . Cameron is tough . . . brilliant . . . while David Cameron wears his leadership lightly, he carries a very big stick . . . old-fashioned army officer insouciance . . . stunning . . . plausible . . . incredibly impressive . . . a fighter . . . a winner . . .'

I should, in fairness, point out that those are my dots.

Jordan now being rich enough to buy General Motors following its share crash

As in the day you read some article in the paper about how Jordan is faring in the recession (pretty well, apparently – loads of book and telly cash), but think little of it . . .

Then you see on the evening news that the General Motors share price has crashed to a level that's amazingly only 10 per cent of its previous highs – and you think: Hmm, Jordan could probably buy General Motors. Outright, in cash. You know, if she wanted to . . . But then you think no more about it . . .

Later on, post-divorce, I was initially impressed with how Katie Price maintained her dignity. Then she went to

Ibiza, on a massive booze bender, flashing her knickers, gyrating on a podium, with broken glass and champagne all over the floor, with the staff trying to clean it up with tissue paper, and she was alleged to have told one female reporter: 'I'll cut your fucking face!' With some of her friends attacking a man, pushing him against a wall, kicking him and trying to gouge his eyes. With one fan asking her for a picture and being refused with Ms Price saying: 'Another thing, I should let you know that you're ugly. Really ugly.' Then she 'begged for sex 15 times an hour' (!) and Twittered about Pete only having an 'acorn'.

Fair enough, you might think. As did I. But then I got angry. It's all very well reverting back to your so-called 'Jordan' alter ego, I thought, but WHAT ABOUT THE CAR WORKERS? These guys don't know if they've got a job next week, and you're pissing yourself stupid up several walls, woman!

Then I remembered she hadn't actually bought General Motors.

Then I wondered: Had she, though?

Then I couldn't remember.

I imagine she's probably much the same.

Jordan: tourist attraction

When Canadian comedy actor Seth Rogen came to Britain to promote the film *Observe and Report*, he told the press he was looking forward most of all to seeing 'that girl . . . with the biggest breasts in the universe . . . You know who I mean. Dawn, is it?'

Journalists (British journalists: best journalists in the world) quickly established that he meant Jordan.

'Can you believe I've never seen them?' Rogen added, incredulously.

However, and this is ironic, at that time the pre-split Jordan was in America filming *Katie and Peter: Stateside*. That's just how it is, Seth – tits can travel in both directions. Sorry.

Juice bar economy getting juiced, The

Tell the people of the future about juice bars and they won't believe you. No really, there were these bars selling drinks that cost the best part of a fiver but which didn't get you remotely pissed, and some of the drinks were even made from grass. Those were the most expensive drinks – the ones made from grass. That was 'juice bars' for you. Really the juice was just something to cut through all the coffee we used to drink in those days. We practically pissed coffee.

Then one day: gone, gone, gone. Okay, it's not the greatest tragedy in the world. There are harder stories out there. The heart has not been ripped out of the communities these juice bars once served. But it is a story of our times. How we used to drink plastic pint-pots absolutely *full* of juice.

In the States, they even had nude juice bars. They're probably still doing okay.

K

Kebabs

Apparently, a vegan SUV driver has a lower carbon footprint than a cycling meat-eater. So that's good news for drivers of vegan SUVs, less good news for those who ride bikes while eating meat – but we always knew that lot were trouble.

According to a report by the Committee on Climate Change, it turns out lambs are the worst bastards of all – which is one in the eye for those who thought it was cows. They're not just out there baaa-ing, they're also burping: burping devil-gas into the biosphere. Baaaa!

Wouldn't it have been great if kebabs were actually good for the environment? Clearly, that was never going to happen. But a climate change scientist declaring: 'Science says, eat more kebabs'? That would have put a smile on my face. And a kebab in my mouth.

But no. And, in my heart of hearts, I guess I did know.

Maybe there should be an awareness campaign:

'Do your bit, lay off the spit.'

'A doner for dinner makes you an environmental sinner.'

'Don't eat shish, it's even worse than fish.'

'If you don't want the planet to continue getting shitter, order something vegetarian (like hummus or falafel) to put inside your pitta.'

Sadly the report did not give a line on Kebabulous, the father and son topless Greek *Riverdancing* duo off *Britain's Got Talent*. Until we hear otherwise, let's assume they are okay for the environment.

Keep Calm And Carry On

You can now get 'Keep Calm And Carry On' everything: cufflinks, hoodies, doormats, deckchairs, posters, dog jackets, baby clothes, flasks, cups, mugs, glasses, books. Keeping calm and carrying on is so fashionable that I was wondering about getting 'Keep Calm And Carry On' shaved into my hair, but then I thought this might be slightly over the top, and could even encourage people to stop keeping calm and carrying on.

The original poster comes from the war of course, although it was never used as it was going to be wheeled out in the event of a Nazi invasion. Which is an almost perfect parallel to a banking crisis. Well, maybe not a *perfect* parallel.

What the author of the poster has done there is employ ironic understatement. Keep calm, the Nazis are here. See? Say what you like about the Nazis, but their invasions were seldom calm affairs. 'Don't pay attention to the Blitzkrieg, Mable, *that's what they want.*'

The idea now is to drum a bit of stoic wartime spirit into us. Funnily enough, Gordon Brown saying that 'the spirit of the Blitz will save us' in the recession coincided with the discovery of a luxury bomb shelter under a hotel in the swanky St James's area of London. The wine cellar was all kitted out with, er, wine and gambling facilities. While the people were initially left almost entirely unprotected, and broke into the Tube stations to take shelter, the elite were sitting pretty. Sort of like the bankers' bonuses of that epoch. But bankers' bonuses that stopped you getting your fucking head blown off. You could just get off your head instead.

Fuck keeping calm. It's rubbish. Even when there was a war on, they were taking the piss. Now there isn't even a war on. (Obviously excepting the war that is on.)

Speaking of war, on Culture Club's 1984 hit 'The War Song', Boy George famously claimed that war is stupid and people are stupid. He later went on to prove this by chaining a man to a wall. That's not *directly* relevant, but still: a lesson for us all there.

Anyway, wasn't it partly to do with people buying too many cufflinks, hoodies, doormats, deckchairs, posters, dog jackets, baby clothes, flasks, cups, mugs, glasses and books that's supposed to have got us into this mess? The recession I mean, not the Nazis. Or being chained to a wall.

Kettling-lite

The Metropolitan Police's controversial tactic of 'kettling' – keeping peaceful protesters locked in a confined space for hours without drinking water or toilet facilities – has been mistaken by many as an attack on the public's right to protest.

Yes, it's detaining people, for protesting. But – and this is the crucial point the nay-sayers seem to miss – during their detention, they are perfectly able to carry on protesting. Don't these people *like* protesting or something? It's not like they're being smacked round the face with shields. Oh no, hang on . . .

Anyway, reviewing the problems with the policing of the G20 demonstration, the Commons' Joint Committee on Human Rights expressed concerns, with chairman Andrew Dismore MP saying: 'While kettling may be a helpful tactic, it can trap peaceful protesters and innocent bystanders for hours.'

Yes, it can, can't it! Trapping peaceful protesters: this *can* be a side-effect of, er, trapping peaceful protesters . . . In future, to avoid undue discomfort or irritation, the committee kindly suggested perhaps providing water and toilet facilities . . .

It really makes you wonder if these people know what they're fucking doing. This is no time for nambying around. You're either a) attacking civil liberties using bizzaro all-encompassing 'anti-terrorism' legislation that seems to let you do anything from stop and searching young Asians to sequestrating the assets of Icelandic banks (fact), or you're b) letting people protest. You really can't combine the two: attacking people's civil liberties while also trying to ensure they don't suffer undue discomfort or irritation over the whole detainment thing. It's the Big Brother who really *cares*.

'Hmm, even with the portaloos, they still might get bored . . . Maybe we could get a café-bar going, lay on some sounds. Hey – we could make money out of this . . .'

L

Labour rebels

Early June 2009. Brown was staggering, nearly on the ground. His authority was crumbling. The government was a void. Every day there were daily bombshells. Could he last the week? The hour, even? Brown was visibly reeling. He really was all over the shop.

Members of the government, the so-called 'Labour rebels', were upping sticks and hitting the streets. Pretty soon, there would be nobody left in the Cabinet and it would become some magic realist fable about the government that wasn't there.

When Work and Pensions Secretary James Purnell quit, commentators asked: 'Is this the fatal blow for Gordon Brown?' It wasn't, for the simple reason that no one gives a toss about James Purnell.

And his friend Miliband? Was David Miliband even a rebel? If he was, he would be the biggest of the rebels – the titanic rebel leader. Immoveable. Unsackable. Miliband. If he was a rebel.

For a few hours, David Miliband did hold Brown's fate in his hand. Would he follow Purnell? In the event, no. He did consider resigning, he later revealed, but then Peter Mandelson told him not to.

Hazel Blears resigned to spend more time at the cut-and-thrust grassroots coalface with her beloved Salford constituents. Although hopefully not the middle-aged female constituent filmed on *Newsnight*, saying: 'I hate her face, I really do. I hate her. I hate her face.' Spending more time with that constituent would not be good for either of them.

So why were these rebels actually rebelling? Er, don't know. I mean, they thought Brown was crap, but is that a cause? Caroline Flint resigned, complaining that she was treated as mere 'window-dressing' – she wasn't just some silly girl! Although the main reason for going did seem to be 'because her mates were doing it'.

Flint's ministerial career had hardly set the world alight, her most famous moment being when she banned biscuits at the Foreign Office. 'The Biscuit Banner' – that was her. A 'Labour insider' told the *Mail*: 'She has a reputation for talking up her own prospects. She had only been Housing Minister for five minutes when it was put about that she wanted to be Transport Secretary. No one has a God-given right to be a Secretary of State.' What, not even when they've slavishly toed the line and assiduously elbowed their way to the front? It must have been her turn – there was no one else left!

With Blears and Flint (and also Jacqui Smith, who resigned because her husband liked porn), the press conjured a hubbly, bubbly coven of witchy assassins – WAGs (Women Against Gordon) – which was probably sexist, but also far more interesting than the truth.

Was there *any* actual politics going on here? Not particularly. Paxman asked backbench rebel leader Barry

Sheerman directly what policies he favoured. 'Ah, well . . . yes . . . Ah,' he said. Before gamely having a go with: 'Sometimes I think we've got *too many* policies.'

In the end, Brown was saved by Labour doing really, really badly in the local and European elections. The period after the elections was a tumultuous twenty-four hours. And yet, at the same time, really quite boring. And what of Miliband? Eventually, he revealed: 'We don't want a new leader.' Translation: 'We don't want me. Even I don't want me . . .'

But the most striking image remains Blears' 'ROCKING THE BOAT' brooch, showing a cat and a dog rocking a boat on a silver sea under the light of a crescent moon. The one she wore when she went off to rock Brown's boat. She came to regret that brooch. Particularly when it transpired that she might be de-selected from her seat for undermining the party during an election campaign, so contributing to the election of Britain's first BNP MEPs.

'Sorry about the brooch,' Blears said.

London 2012 fatigue

God, I'm bored of the Olympics. It's not happening for *years* and still my head aches with it.

Look, it's just a total pain in the arse and the UK could probably find better uses for the money. Unsurprisingly, Boris Johnson is comparing these Games not with Beijing 2008, but with London 1948. Which had far fewer fireworks (they would have made people jumpy).

His first money-scrimping wheeze was not to bother

with a bespoke fourteen-thousand-seater basketball sta-dium, instead holding the sport in the existing Wembley Arena. But soon a serious problem was uncovered: the dressing rooms at the venue, normally host to pint-sized pop stars (they were actually designed for Kylie Minogue), were too small for seven-foot-plus men-mountains. The cost of raising the ceilings was so prohibitive that they decided to build the new basketball stadium anyway. Did no one think of digging a hole in the floor, though?

A smaller stadium, pencilled in for the badminton, was also temporarily axed, when someone questioned whether badminton is even played at the Olympics. Well, is it? Did they do some in Beijing? No one could remember. One person could recall watching some yngling, whatever that is. But not badminton. Anyway, a six-thousand-seater's going up, just in case.

Exactly what is all the panic about, though? In 2009, extensive research shows there are two running tracks already built in London and its immediate environs. There are probably loads more, but as you only need one, that's when I stopped counting. So that's £496 million for the main stadium saved in one fell swoop.

What else? A swimming pool? Councils are *always* boast-ing about having an 'Olympic-sized swimming pool' – what is the point in having one of those, if not for the Olympics? Olympic village: maybe they could check on the Internet about that, just type in 'London' and 'hotels' and see if anything comes up? And we live on an island, so there's plenty of water around to hold the yngling. Whatever that turns out to be. Let's just not bother with badminton this time round.

And have the IOC let darts in yet? My local pub's got a board you can have, if someone else whacks a nail in the wall.

Looming enviro-catastrophe being 'good for Britain'

We'll be okay. Barbecue summers all round for us Brits. The barbecue summers we're often promised will, come global warming proper, be a fairly safe bet for the Met Office. So that's the future: loads of dads running around with tongs and charcoal and rosé and meat, getting all excited about cooking meat. The future is a happy garden. Let it bloom. And you can stop thinking of the North Sea in a dark way, all watery grey doom (brrr). That's the new Med, that is (aaah). Bridlington shall rise again. Well, maybe not Bridlington. But other places.

Okay, so scientists are claiming the need to convert to low carbon and so save the world from runaway climate change is beyond urgent – but for us, here in sunny Britain, what's the rush? We're not Tuvalu! Britain is one of the 'lifeboat nations' – along with Canada and Siberia and Tasmania and a few other places – where everyone else wishes they'd been born. (Yes, people will wish they had been born in Siberia. It's well clement.)

In one piece eulogising a leading climate change sceptic (it must be so much easier to become a leading climate change sceptic now there are so few of them), *Spectator* writer James Delingpole wondered what the fucking problem was, lauding lovely warm summer days and opining that 'the earth's warmer periods – such as when the Romans grew grapes and citrus trees as far north as Hadrian's Wall – were times of wealth and plenty.'

Ah yes, the Roman Empire. Bet *they* put on a good barbecue: char-grilled meats followed by a big group shag. Maybe that's what we should be thinking of getting back to. Drinking Geordie wine. Palm trees and pistachios. Throwing another shark on the grill. You can almost hear the lyres and the laughter. Bit of a shame about the millions of refugees at the gates . . . but then, some people are just born lucky, I guess.

And, oh, my invite must have got lost in the post. Even if Britain is going to be one long barbecue (aside from the storms, flash floods, malaria, etc., which can disrupt even the best-organised barbecues), who's invited? Okay, global elites don't want to hang out in Northumberland *now*, but wait until Northumberland is a veritable paradise. Rich people coming in and buying up all the houses so other people don't have anywhere to live? Does that sound like the sort of thing that could happen in Britain?

Everything privatised and skewed to benefit the ultra-wealthy? Does *that* sound like the sort of thing that could happen in Britain? Already, around the world, rich elites are boxing off food supplies, and water supplies, and there's a Chinese and Saudi-powered 'land grab' of arable land in Africa. Come on, you must have seen *Quantum of Solace*!

A country struggling to feed itself because it relies on imports that are no longer there, with the countryside dotted with biofuel and power-generation projects that don't work, because the politicians were lobbied by their mates? In Britain? Britain? Really? So it'll be like, er, that Bond film with all the biofuel projects that don't work.

So unless things change in really quite a dramatic fashion, when climate chaos starts roaring in our faces like a bastard, it's going to be one scarily exclusive barbecue, with the super-rich guests being flown in on armed helicopters, the perimeter fence guarded by privatised hounds dripping saliva from their terrifying serrated teeth of death, the grill itself manned by semi-fascists in aviator shades, any unwanted prowlers fleeing the tribal barbarism being thrown into a private cell – and all for a mangy sausage made out of fetid horsemeat. A really, really bleak barbecue surrounded by hunger, thirst and fire-damaged scrub.

Of course, it might not turn out that bad. They may have proper sausages. It's hard to predict at this point.

Love on the dole

Hitherto people thought most adultery happened at work. But no. Take away the distraction of being at work and thus having to do work, and everyone starts realising how randy they feel.

Apparently, sites like Illicitencounters.com are booming. Ex-bankers are often meeting up with former colleagues for a quick drink. In their former colleague's bedroom. Without any clothes on. The construction industry too: builders are now spending their days actually having if off rather than talking about having it off. So 'I'd give her one' has now become 'I have actually given her one'. Or 'him', even.

The US-based Ashley Madison dating agency saw membership soar from 1 million to 3.6 million after it launched a series of daytime TV ads using the slogan: 'Life is short. Have an affair.'

On Craigslist, one recently redundant young man even tried to raise his spirits by offering London ladies a 'credit munch' – presumably, he was also remembering the importance of using downtime to mug up on key skills.

But it's not all recession humping boomtime. It's tough times for private investigators, as wronged spouses are doing much of the surveillance legwork themselves. PI John Dinitale, interviewed on CNN, has seen business drop off by 75 per cent. He also reported that illicit partners are forgoing expensive restaurants and hotel-rooms for bunk-ups in cars or the park.

It's tough times for lawyers, too, as people are deciding they can't afford to get divorced. They just, you know, fuck in the park all day to take their minds off things. Resourceful, humans, aren't they?

M

Damian McBride having the nickname 'Mad Dog'

Now, we've all sent embarrassing emails. You know the ones. The ones where, as soon as you've pressed 'SEND', you immediately think, Oh fuck-a-duck, I really shouldn't have done that. The ones that skirt legality by indicating ways of spreading malicious slander claiming that political rivals are up to bad sex. Those ones. Or that David Cameron had the clap. Stuff like that.

It's all part of the fun at Gordon Brown's Cunts' Camelot, though. Smeargate ringleader Damian McBride wasn't just part of Brown's Westminster clan, he was Brown's bastard – a big old bastard nicknamed Mad Dog. He has additionally been called 'Brown's Rasputin', although that role has also been attributed to Charlie Whelan. Unless Brown had two Rasputins? (Christ, *two* Russian mystic-priest philanderers in the house?)

Political wisdom states that everyone needs a bastard. Do they, though? Imagine if we all had our own bastards. I mean, I'd quite like a bastard for a bit, to see what it was like . . . but anyway, what sort of person has the nickname Mad Dog? Let me think . . . well, there's Loyalist paramilitary Johnny 'Mad Dog' Adair whose feud with fellow Loyalists over his alleged drug-dealing forced him to move to England and hang out with white supremacists. That's pretty mad.

And there's Damian 'Mad Dog' McBride, the Prime Minister's (former) Head of Strategy and Planning. 'I've got a strategy, right – it's barking at the fucking moon, yeah? Owwwwwww! That's me barking at the moon, yeah? What are *you* fucking laughing at? I'm talking to you, bollocks . . .'

Ironically, McBride's accomplice Derek Draper is also some sort of psycho-healer. So maybe he was just trying to be empathetic and humble. After all, it's no good holding these things in. Much better to let it all out – via Internet scandal-sheets.

Draper is, of course, married to GMTV's Kate Garraway. Fair enough. But at the time of the email scandal, she was all over the front of the frothy mags talking about her new slimming show on ITV, and makeovers and stuff. Whatever, but it must have made for some pretty fucked-up chats over the breakfast table.

'What are you doing today, Derek? I'm doing a photo-shoot in a beautiful summer field to promote my new slimming show on ITV.'

'Cool, I'm going to circulate some really dark insinuations about people being mental. I might not be home for dinner.'

Madonna's African baby-buying, Outcry over

What, so you can't just go and buy kids you like the look of these days? Without people hitting the shit on you? 'Bleuh,

bleuh, who do you think you are, flashing your money round, blah blah blah?' It's not like she hasn't done it before. Get over it.

I do worry about the little ones, though, I really do. Growing up to realise that their adoptive mother is someone who seems remarkably prone to parting her legs, really quite widely, in public. On telly. While wearing a leotard.

Kids hate that shit.

Making your own clothes

It's the Holy Grail of self-sanctifying self-reliance – seeing if you can bring in an outfit for less than an Asian sweatshop.

Great. Mind you, have you ever bought wool? It's far more expensive than you can possibly imagine. So walking round in some bride-of-Frankenstein monstrosity you've somehow conjured out of two hundred quids' worth of wool: that's going to help, is it?

And where have the curtains gone?

Manchester City's upturn in fortunes after becoming world's richest club, Prospect of

In 2008, Manchester City Football Club was taken over by an Abu Dhabi consortium headed by Sheikh Mansour bin Zayed Al Nahyan, the man with the keys to the executive washroom at Oil plc. Jubilant City fans celebrated by wearing towels on their heads. Nice.

Bin Zayed Al Nahyan's purchase of the club made City,

at a stroke, the richest in the world. Which means that, if cash really is everything, they could soon be the best team in the world. As of now, we have no way of knowing whether the plan will work. All we *can* say is take a look at City's history:

1. In 1936/37, City win the League Championship for the very first time.
2. A year later, they become the first reigning champions to be relegated. Nobody else has managed this since.
3. In 1967/68, they win the league for the second time.
4. This is overshadowed two weeks later by Manchester United, who win the European Cup.
5. Manchester City try to emulate their neighbours' success in the 1968/69 European Cup.
6. City are knocked out of the 1968/69 European Cup in the first round.
7. In 1995/96, drawing at Liverpool in the final game of the season, City manager Alan Ball orders his players to waste time during the last few minutes, as a draw will be enough to ensure they avoid relegation.
8. Except it isn't.
9. And they don't.
10. Oasis become the club's most famous fans. This is the hardest blow of all if you are a City fan, as everyone assumes you are the sort of person who likes Oasis.
11. City are bought out by Thai PM Thaksin

Shinawatra, which pleases City fans, even though he is clearly one murky dude whose war on drugs involved extra-judicial killing sprees. Thaksin employs Sven-Göran Eriksson, and in 2007/08 watches the Swede's side embark on the club's most promising start to a league campaign since 1972.

12. The club's most promising start to a league campaign since 1972 ends with an 8-1 defeat at Middlesbrough. Manchester United win the European Cup.

It doesn't augur well, really. But things can change, people can change, institutions can change. And, now they've got rid of Shinawatra, Amnesty International are back onside. Providing they haven't seen that video allegedly showing Mansour bin Zayed Al Nahyan's brother beating someone with a poker and setting fire to his balls.

That's his real balls.

Manure lagoons

After swine flu emerged in the Veracruz area of Mexico, it didn't take long before scientists were pointing to the existence of an enormous pig factory-farm in the region, run by US agrobusiness giant Smithfield Foods, the largest pork producer on the planet. When it comes to pigs, these guys are the hogs. Boss Hog – that's what these guys could call themselves.

Smithfield take thousands upon thousands upon thousands of pigs, fill them full of drugs and cram so many into vast spaces that their excrement creates, literally, lakes of shit – vast lakes of shit that provide ideal conditions for bacteria to breed. The industry prefers to call them 'manure lagoons', which sounds like something out of a holiday brochure (albeit a really fucked up one).

The World Health Organization has been warning of a pig-related pandemic for some years. Big lakes of shit. How did they turn out to be not a good idea? It's got success written all over it. Or not. You don't have to be a biologist to posit that nothing good comes out of a lake of shit.

Even wine lakes are bad, apparently. So shit lakes are definitely a no-no.

Marks & Spencer saving the planet

M&S, when not using oozy-voiced sex-ads to insinuate that its food is dirty – not unclean dirty, dirty like a whore; filthy food that will get up to anything – is always going on about being the greenest retailer.

But M&S stores are populated with row after row of chiller cabinets set to 'fucking freezing' and chock full of ready meals, so that's just bollocks really, isn't it?

There is presumably some food in these aisles. But you can't see it because of all the paper and plastic. They could be selling plastic boxes with pictures of food on, for all you can actually tell.

Maybe they've worked out a cunning way to produce ready meals, put them in paper and plastic, then transport them around the country in chilled vans, to sit in chilled aisles awaiting a chilled purchase, in a way that is environmentally beneficial, to the environment. But they don't seem *that* clever. Not defying-physics clever, anyway.

But let us not be churlish. According to the *Guardian*, M&S boss Stuart Rose has got green initiatives 'coming out of his ears', which even *sounds* green. (Stuart Rose was born to lead M&S. Is there a more M&S name than *Stuart Rose*?) After a damascene viewing of *An Inconvenient Truth*, he and his fellow managers set about establishing Plan A (as in, there is no Plan B), an M&S action plan to save the world.

Scanning the Plan A website, you'll see it involves things like switching to M&S for your gas and electricity, and making sure to cook *all* the food you buy in M&S rather than, say, throwing it all in the bin. (Just throw the plastic and cardboard and Clingfilm bits in the bin. Don't throw the individually packed exotic side-salads of the world themselves in the bin.)

There is some gubbins about how they always ask their suppliers to turn the lights off in their factories at night, but mainly Plan A seems to be geared towards buying things in and from M&S. Buy more stuff: that's the message here. Buy more M&S stuff.

Rose explained: 'I'll be absolutely clear, we're running a commercial business. Just like with the "Flown" labels on the peas. I am not going to stop offering customers peas out of season, all right? I'm going to put them into stores. But what I am going to do, is I am going to put a label on them, saying I've flown them. Right? Let the customer make the choice. You want to eat fresh peas? Let your conscience know that they have been flown.

'On the other hand, you don't want to eat peas, you want to eat turnips, because they're in season? Fine. That's your choice.

'Although of course it is much more complicated than that.'

Probably is.

It also turned out to be more complicated than Rose imagined to buy the hydrogen-powered BMW which emits water vapour, the one he told all the media he was getting – there was, like, a waiting list or something – so he made do with a succession of Bentleys and use of the M&S private plane.

Maybe that's what he means when he says of out-of-season peas, 'I am going to put a label on them, saying I've flown them' – that he *himself* has flown all the peas, individually, in the M&S private plane? Stranger things have happened at M&S, believe it or not.

Mayfair's own 'ground zero'

Did you know there's a ground zero in London? Don't bother going. It's rubbish. No one selling any baseball caps or anything.

Okay, so it's not the sight of a terrorist-spectacular mass grave – but for many this site is the meltdown's 'own ground zero . . . the hottest point . . . the epicentre', the point from which the devastation fanned out. A very dark place indeed. It is, not to put too fine a point on it, the office of an insurance company.

In the normal run of things, when people say they are going into insurance, you don't reply: 'Well, good luck to you. I've heard it's one hell of a ride.' But AIG was an insurance company gone bad.

The fifth floor of One Curzon Street, Mayfair, was where the US insurance giant based its notorious Financial Products team. AIG has been called a 'renegade' insurance company, with the maddest wing of all – run by multi-millionaire 'genius' Joseph Cassano – being the Mayfair office, where they could get away with all sorts of dirty stuff not even allowed by the Bush administration. The company's Stateside HQ called it 'the casino in London'. So, it was renegade insurance guys in a casino. And you know what that's like.

In common with no other rational human who has ever stepped inside a casino, these guys believed they had abolished risk. In 2007, Cassano told one analyst: 'It is hard for us, without being flippant, to even see a scenario within any kind of realm of reason that would see us losing one dollar.'

In a way, he was right. When it all came crashing down, the company posted the greatest quarterly losses in American corporate history: $61.7 billion. Which is 'not losing a dollar' by some distance.

One US Congressman voiced the anger of many, saying that the American public understood that 'AIG stood for Arrogance, Incompetence and Greed.' (If this was true, and the initials 'AIG' really did stand for those things, this would represent a truly shocking oversight by the regulatory authorities.)

So it was just a few mad bastards who ruined it for

everyone? Er, not so much. Everyone else was in the casino too. It was a really kicking casino that saw the high-street banks getting really hooked with anyone even suggesting the wheels were obviously going to fall off – that it was time to stop drinking and go home – being made to look like a stupid square.

Paul Moore, the Head of Group Regulatory Risk at HBOS, analysed the riskiness of their adventures and warned his bosses of an imminent smash-up. He was promptly fired and replaced with someone from Sales. But . . . Moore was the *risk guy*! If you didn't want to hear about the risk, don't even *have* a risk guy. Just say, you know what? Let's not even *have* a risk guy, we could use the space for another jukebox.

His boss at HBOS was James Crosby, at this point both Gordon Brown's favourite banker and the Deputy Chair of the Financial Services Authority – the industry police who, it turns out, didn't give a fuck about risk, despite giving a fuck about risk being one clear reason for their very existence.

So the police were high on the risk. And so were the umpires. The big three credit rating companies – Standard & Poor's, Moody's and Fitch Ratings – seemed to rate their debt-bundles like they thought complex bundles of debt were somehow connected to everlasting orgasms. Not just one A, not just two As, but three As! Three As! Triple-A! A times three! A! A! Aaaaa! (And who was it who paid them for all this good work? It was the banks.) Even when the RBS business model went tits up to the tune of billions, Moody's took urgent action and stripped the stricken bank of its Triple-A rating. Well, that only seemed fair. Predicting billions more write-downs to come, they knocked them right down to, erm ... AA1. Christ on a fucking bike, what would you have to do to get a C? Blow yourself up in the meetings?

Later revelations of emails between ratings company analysts indicated that they knew they were wildly over-rating the debt-structures but were still having a high old time, so who cares? One analyst said: 'It could be structured by cows and we would rate it.'

Don't bring the cows into this, you bastards.

Middle-class rioters

There is a spectre haunting Europe, suggested the Met in early 2009: middle-class rioters 'playing the role Marx conceived for the proletariat'. People in Boden outfits, fucking the place up.

Although, actually, this didn't happen. So either a) the whole 'middle-class rioter' thing was just a bit of cash-raising alarmism dreamed up by those very special people at the Met. Or b) it hasn't happened *yet*. If house prices take a further tumble, look out for someone in a balaclava setting up barricades, a crèche and a first-aid tent.

'To the front. You've got to get to the front, Jasmine. How will you ever get smashed in the face by the police and become the bloodied poster-girl for the international fight-back if you hang around at the back? And for God's sake stand up straight ...'

Mistresses

It's all just too realistic. I was only after some easy escapism. But drinking wine while standing up? Wondering if they even fancy men any more? Having emotional crises while drinking ice-cold Pinot Grigio, standing up? That's my life, that is.

Shagging the son of your married lover who you just put to sleep for ever? That's me all over. Well, it could have been. I'm like that.

Organising a wedding for a lesbian couple then switching sexual sides to sleep with one half of the couple? While drinking Pinot? I might as well just look in the mirror.

Filling the hole left by your 9/11 victim husband with a possible psycho? Been there, done that.

Although possibly even I would take a couple of days off now and then before lurching headlong into my next glossy but self-destructive emotional maelstrom.

Also, why not try some red wine for a change? Sitting down, even?

Money Shop, The

Like ladies? Like money? Feeling horny? For cash? You're in the right place: it's The Money Shop – the sexiest shop in town. Except for the sex shop.

The Money Shop is the only place to head when you're feeling really, really randy and desperate for cash. The boards in the street outside show highly coquettish young women pouting at passers-by like they're proffering loan-related blowjobs. Here's a ravishing wide-eyed brunette without any clothes on, but covering her breasts with cash money. 'Let's Talk Cash!' she implores. (I'd talk cash with you any day – overdrafts, homeowner loans, all sorts . . . We could look at some price-comparison websites. Oh yeah.)

There she is again, in the window, still topless, but now covered in gold jewellery – because 'there's never been a better time to trade your gold'. That's your gold she's wearing. Okay, she hasn't paid top whack for it – but she has put it on her tits. She might wear your fillings too if you ask her nicely. In the buff. Oh yeah.

Also in the window, there's a poster of a hunky young lad being asked: 'What would £1000 bring you?' Looking up into a dream bubble, he sees himself, fanning out a big wad of dollars and euros. He's grinning and wearing shades with a lovely, lovely lady-friend on his arm. Look at that crazy, happy guy. He's getting his holiday shags in. So could you. Get in there now for a 212 per cent payday loan before you cash that cheque all over yourself.

Sex sells. You know it. But in The Money Shop the thing that sex sells is money. Which is weird. It's a strange sort of selling where you have to give it back, along with your watch. Wonder what the returns policy is? 'Look, I bought this money here last week. Sorry, but it's not working for me, I want my money back . . .' Still, shagging though: great.

'Most viewed' stories on Internet news pages

1. Man bites snake in epic struggle
2. 'Bone voyage' as pets get airline

3. People may be able to taste words
4. 24 hours to stave off global meltdown
5. Secret Susan Boyle song found
6. Loving horses will die together
7. Quick thinking averts near cat-astrophe
8. 'Giant' hedgehog forced to diet
9. Girl with fifty-six stars tattooed on face admits she asked for them
10. Man complains his pizza has no topping – until he realises it is upside down

MPs

Personally, I could not believe what the MPs had been up to. I didn't believe it and in some ways I still don't. The expenses scandal was an amazing time for British democracy, the greatest democracy in the world. There were daily revelations – and who doesn't like their revelations to come daily? (Albeit not necessarily *every* day for six months.)

Still, if you are going to have a scandal that calls into question the very concept of democracy, it might as well be funny. And it was. Duck houses! Ha ha! Loo seats! Prescott on the crapper! Ha ha ha! Blue movies? What a laugh.

The whole thing went on for so long that it became increasingly difficult to work out which claims were real and which you'd made up in the pub a few weeks before. Did the famously very rich Labour (and former Tory) MP Shaun Woodward really claim for a Crunch Corner yoghurt? Or was this part of some post-five-pint pub game? If your MP claimed for a Cadbury's Animal Bar, which Cadbury's Animal Bar would he or she claim for? Do you remember that game? A great game. My MP would claim for the frog, deffo.

Did Gerald Kaufman claim for a £225 biro and David Davis £2500 for the upkeep of a paddock? Were Tony Blair's expenses 'accidentally' shredded, in a shredding incident? You know, I can't quite recall. But yes. Did Lembit Opik claim for a wig? Yes, he did: twice! The Mother of All Wigs and a Filmstar wig – to wear at a charitable event (and then afterwards in the bedroom).

Unbelievable, really. Although, having said that, these are the people who voted for the Iraq War without a second thought. And who had been cheerleading City 'inventiveness'. And who voted through the steady privatisation of the NHS. These people had already fucked up more than one brain can feasibly take in at one time, and had – bar some honourable exceptions (i.e., about twenty) – at no point shown themselves to be anything other than greedy, gutless freaks. So I say it was unbelievable, but maybe, when I think about it, it *is* actually believable. MPs? A bunch of greedy, gutless freaks, you say? Well, I've never thought of it that way before, but now that you mention it, that would make some sense.

Still, we were on to them now. And nothing would ever be the same again. Although are we absolutely sure *nothing* will be the same again? Because it does still feel a bit the same again. There's not really a huge amount going on here, is there? I'm sure I would have noticed. I mean, I saw people getting baity on *Question Time*. And one angry voter interviewed on the news saying he was so disillusioned with the main parties that he was 'considering voting Green ... or UKIP!' (Because who doesn't find it hard to tell those two apart? Rabid Europhobes? Environmentalists? Environmentalists? Rabid Europhobes?)

In the main, it was: I'm going to be angry about something very specific, and just for today. As if people were most angry about having to be bothered with the whole question of politics at all. Fucking hell, I voted three years ago, why are you bothering me again *now*, for fuck's sake?

All that other shit, we can kind of put up with: the government automatically getting a third of the votes because all the ministers, parliamentary private secretaries, etc. have to vote with them; the chairs of all the committees that oversee the government being appointed by, er, the government; only getting to vote every five years without any power of recall if you realise you've made a dreadful mistake; former public health ministers getting consultancies with private health companies; everyone getting consultancies with everyone; the make-up of Parliament looking as much like the make-up of the general population as a blue balloon on a fucking stick; a general feeling that the world is run by and for someone else. All fine. But a fucking duck island? A *duck island*! This I will not stand!

Okay, the expenses do make it worse. Knowing that your MP nodded through a couple of conflicts while energetically thinking up ways to claim for the re-grouting of their cousin's mate's downstairs toilet: that's worse. But there's definitely more to life than bathplugs. Yes, without one, the water all flows out. But for *fuck's sake*.

Of course, the defence of 'the system' was that MPs need to top up their salary with expenses because they don't get paid nearly enough. Although this 'not nearly enough' is still £67,000 a year, which does put them in the top 3 per cent of the country's earners. The male median wage in Britain – that is, the most common wage, the one that more people get paid than get paid any greater or lesser wage – is about £25,000. That, I'd say, is not enough. £67,000? That probably is enough.

So maybe people who won't do the job for £67,000 simply aren't that interested in representing people, or in people generally. Maybe politics isn't for them? Maybe anyone who does want to make loads of cash could consider – you know, just consider – fucking off to do something else?

Ah yes, but it's not just that: people earning £67,000 cannot be expected to mix convincingly with business leaders. The real movers and shakers would just laugh at them and their shitty £67,000 rations if they didn't also tuck in to the system to get a bit more. (Twice as much more, or three times as much, if at all possible.)

Although I can't help thinking that these elected officials were getting their roles mixed up here: when mixing with businesspeople, weren't they supposed to be representing the interests of the rest of the people? Whereas it sometimes, usually even, looked like they were representing the interests of the businesspeople . . . as opposed to the rest of the people. Unfortunately, we have recently been experiencing how this process ends up: we hand over the freehold on hospitals, they bankrupt the country. Oopsy-fucking-daisy.

In a final irony, as a result of the wave of 'retirements' hitting the Commons before the next election, power is likely to get *more* centralised, with anyone with a bit of nous shoved aside for a fifteen-year-old appointed by central office. So, as a result of the scandal, the House of Commons may well get even less democratic than before. It's almost enough to make you think we should start looking into what we hope to get out of this whole 'politics' thing anyway.

Sir Peter Viggers auctioned the duck island for charity, you know. So yes, even after everything else, he went and made the ducks homeless. Unbelievable, really.

Quack quack.

Myersons at war

Which side were you on? The mother parading her son's private pain round the media? Or the teenager always punching his dad in the face? It was a conflict that engulfed the world. The trauma is still being felt to this day. In years to come, children will turn to their fathers and ask: 'Daddy, what did you do in the Myersons war?' And their fathers will go very quiet at the memory of what they were forced to endure.

We must never forget. Thank God, then, that now, available for the first time on DVD, is the eleven-disc box set of the acclaimed documentary covering the whole conflict, *Myersons at War*. This was the programme that redefined the gold standard for television documentary. Brilliantly narrated by Laurence Olivier, it remains the benchmark by which all factual programming must judge itself. The result is a unique and unrepeatable event, since many of the eye-witnesses captured on film did not have long left to live.

Originally shown as twenty-six one-hour programmes, it set out to tell the story through the testimony of key participants. Each programme is carefully structured to focus on a key theme or campaign. Includes eyewitness accounts from everyone who ever knew them who also writes a column in a newspaper.

Which is everyone who ever knew them.

And, coming soon: *Myersons at War: In Colour*.

N

Niceness, Rumours of increased

No more bashing up hospital staff with your new Manolos. The recession's here! Come and join our sewing club instead.

We're all going to be better people now – families all eating plates full of fresh herbs around the same table at the same time, the right time: dinner time. Not just going out and getting drunk all the time. Sometimes staying in and getting drunk instead.

Columnist Simon Jenkins predicted families would 'rediscover their hobbies such as sports, stamp collecting and trainspotting'. A fascinating insight for those who thought Simon Jenkins had been beamed in from the 1950s, unless by the last one he meant doing skag and going on about Iggy.

Even online personal finance site the Motley Fool was at it, with an editorial about how we need to put the boom behind us and get back to 'real' things. Although at the very same time it was busy rebranding itself as love-money.com. So maybe they're more confused than they're letting on.

Nihilistic blog responses to George Monbiot articles about the environment

For people who don't find George Monbiot's articles about the environment apocalyptic enough, there are the comments people append to them on the *Guardian*'s website. Here are some recent examples:

marcopolo

With humanity facing a 'triple crunch' of financial crisis, oil running out and runaway climate change, isn't it about time we all woke up to the fact that there is no hope? This is no time for illusions. Or illusionists.

Automaticslim

People who talk about humanity facing a triple crunch of credit, energy and climate are woefully underplaying the scale of the calamity we face. I have counted twelve more crunches that will all combine to guarantee global devastation. I would tell you what they are, but I don't want to. God, you're all so pathetic!

Aynrand4evah

I'm going up to Snowdonia. I'm going to dig a hole. I'm going to get in my hole. I'm going to pull a roof over my hole. And that's what's going to happen to me. I've got a tin cup.

weirddave

I'm sick of all these people kidding themselves that we can possibly do anything to avoid societal collapse. It's going to be like *Day of the Triffids*. Or maybe *The Road*. Or even *Survivors*. Good. I like that sort of thing. *The Road*? That's me.

heffalump

I'm all right. I'm a trained marksman. I'll be able to slaughter all the wildlife in a fifty-mile radius and pick off anyone who enters the same valley. As soon as they clear that thicket, peeeow! Right in the chops! You fuck!

themadun

All these people believing they will survive in an imminent reversion to tribal brutalism are woefully optimistic about the future. Are we all overlooking the fact that without Western medicine everyone will quickly die of smallpox? A pox on you all! Literally!

Tezzah22

So, still clinging to the sad but ultimately calming belief that all life will end suddenly with some outbreak of smallpox or other calamitous infection? If only things turn out that cosily . . .

Holygrail

This romantic idea that planet Earth will carry on okay without us is another sign of the intellectual weakness that mars our species. NASA scientists believe that recently spotted dust particles around burnt-out white dwarf stars are the remains of planets just like ours. That's all your precious planet Earth will be in the end. Get over it, for God's sake.

Dave3

Typical leftist claptrap from Monbiot again. Don't you know it's the cows farting!

9/11 being a bit 'over'

You definitely don't hear as much about it as you used to.

Clash of civilisations? Bollocks! I'm losing money here!

'No one could have predicted this recession', The phrase

Yes, they could. Otherwise there would be no one now saying: 'I told you so.' And there are loads.

Given that the bubble years were totally fucking mentally off their nutjob rocker in just about every conceivable way imaginable, you would hardly have needed to have taken recession studies from the age of five to have accurately predicted the whole credit-bubble hyper-consumerist thing might shake itself to bits at some point.

A fucking monkey could have predicted some sort of 'all the wheels falling off' situation occurring at some point in the near future.

I said it myself. I said: 'This can't last.'

And I was right.

Of course, quite a lot of financial firms couldn't predict the recession because they deliberately built computer models that were unable to predict it. At Lehman Brothers, events that models predicted would happen once every ten thousand years suddenly happened every day for three days. The Goldman Sachs computer daily showed events so unlikely that they should not happen, even if the history of the universe were relived fourteen times over. What are the odds, eh?

The Treasury, though, built computer models that *could*

predict the recession, and *did* predict the recession (they even did war game-style sessions about a credit collapse. But they kept it under their hats hoping it would go away, presumably spending most of their time practising their lines in the mirror: 'NO ONE could have predicted this recession . . . Not I, not you, not him, not her, not anyone . . . or anything could have or did predict this recession . . . or any other recession.'

O

Obamarama

From now on, I'm not doing a thing. No need. The right man is in place. Not like that other idiot – him I did not like. But now Obama's here. And he's talking about change. He's a one-man change machine. Dispensing change for all. Take note of his change.

I just took one look at his wife's arms and I thought – that's the man for me. Adopting a stray puppy just confirmed it. And that is literally all I need to know about the man.

I'm not even going to read news stories to see how he's getting on. That kind of thing isn't even really relevant here. I'm all about trusting Obama to do the right thing. He's a great leader. And if you can't trust a great leader to do the right thing, who can you trust?

I haven't even tidied my house since Obama got in. I'm leaving it. And, okay, I didn't tidy up much when Bush was in power either. But I haven't even tidied it *once* under Obama. And if that's not a sign that I'm giving this thing my all, then I don't know what is.

I mean, I'm not tuning out totally. I've watched him swat that fly on YouTube about a thousand times. And re-watched that off-colour comment about the Special

Olympics – I think he gets away with it myself. And anyway, those guys have had it easy for too long.

And some people say to me, he's reappointed neocons to economic positions, he's up to his gills with various lobbyists, his main adviser is a frothing pro-Israel nutjob who stands on tables and shouts at people, his green policy is a tower of piss built on sand, yada yada yada.

I've never been a big one for listening to some people. I've found increasingly that the best way to listen to some people is not to listen to them. I'm working on a dream here. Quite a dusty dream, maybe; one that involves eating out of cans with my fingers. But it's a dream I'm proud to share with the very many fine people whose lives have been changed in myriad imperceptible ways which only now we are beginning to understand.

Amen.

Ocado van sponsorship

Yes, your family can 'adopt' an Ocado delivery van.

Why? I have absolutely no idea. But they can. Underneath the name of the van (the vans have names!) will be inscribed 'Adopted by the Larkin family from Henley-on-Thames'.

The only rule is that the name of 'your' van has to incorporate one of the following fruits/vegetables: apple, courgette, strawberry, cabbage, lemon or onion.

Why? I have absolutely no idea. Indeed, when I noticed this abominable practice on the side of a van at a pedestrian crossing near my actual home, I was so entirely overtaken with one thought that I had to sit down for a moment, overcome with wondering: WHAT THE FUCK WAS GOING THROUGH THESE PEOPLE'S FUCKING MINDS?!?

Old Spice revival

Apparently, we're in so much need of comfort, we're even craving comfort advertising. The makers of Milky Way spread some love in the recession by re-running vintage ads. Remember those days? The days when you felt safe? Yeah, well we've got some ads that we can re-run for nix about how a Milky Way helps you 'lighten up and play'. Remember those days? When Milky Way and Mars bars provided all the nutrition a growing child could ever require? I miss those days.

They've even had a go at re-launching those classic fragrances *pour homme* Blue Stratos and Old Spice, the latter with the slogan: 'The original. If your grandfather hadn't worn it, you wouldn't exist.' Ah yes, the old smell-like-your-granddad routine. I'm not falling for that one again.

You can even get misty-eyed about how recessions used to be better in the old days. Political journo Andy Beckett wrote a history of the 70s, *When the Lights Go Out*, which challenged standard notions of the decade as a time of untold misery and flared decrepitude: there was even a positive side to the three-day week – only having to work three days a week, for a start. 'Fishing down the canal? Watneys Party Seven? Those were the days. Men were men and you could slap women's arses. What more is there to life?' (Okay, so these are not *exact* quotes from Andy Beckett's history of the 70s.)

In fact, surveys have suggested that people in Britain were indeed at their 'happiest' in the mid-70s, just before the atomised consumer preying-on-dissatisfaction culture got jiggy. Of course, this was also before they took away all the PG Tips monkeys. So maybe it's a bit of both.

George Osborne

George Osborne has been preparing for power. George Osborne is ready for the tough choices that power will entail. Yes, George Osborne is ready . . . for cuts.

Don't worry, though. They won't be normal cuts, cuts as we have hitherto understood them, bad cuts. The Compassionate Conservatives *will* make cuts, but they will make 'caring cuts'.

I think this means they won't be quite so enthusiastic about making cuts as, say, Thatcher – while, as I say, actually making boatloads of cuts. Big boats, too – large enough for Russian oligarchs to hold parties on. Yes, it's a crisis. But isn't a crisis also an opportunity?

Weirdly, despite the anti-state blah-blah, Thatcher and Major increased public spending by an average of 1.5 per cent every year. So thanks to the playing out of Thatcherite ideals – the emptying of the public purse to prop up banks – we will now be facing cuts worse than Thatcher's. When everyone was going on about Tory cuts all the time.

'No more cuts!' That's what people used to shout. On demos. In groups. They only shouted this in groups, on demos. They didn't just shout it out loud in the street.

There were a lot of nutters on the street in those days (partly because of the cuts . . .), but they were usually shouting about other stuff.

But cuts *must* be made – even though cutting public spending in a recession is generally considered the economic equivalent of kicking a one-legged person's leg away (and then robbing them). And George Osborne is ready to make them. In an *FT* interview, he revealed: 'I've mentally adjusted myself and David Cameron has mentally adjusted himself to the fact that we are going to have to take some very difficult decisions for the good of the country.'

They have, together, mentally adjusted themselves – probably physically adjusted themselves too – for cuts. Don't carp. He's spent ages trying occupy the right headspace – kicking back in Corfu, throwing down White Russians with a Rothschild – simply to prepare himself both mentally and indeed emotionally. For cuts.

I can hardly wait to see what they're going to cut first. Libraries? Or pre-school stuff? The NHS frontline? Anyone want to make it interesting? What odds will you give me on the elderly?

By the way, for his expenses, George Osborne claimed for two DVDs of his comments to the Commons on getting value for taxpayers' money. Was he satirising the system with this act? No, he was not.

Michael Owen, Piss Ambassador

In April 2008, oft-injured footballing millionaire and gambler Michael Owen teamed up with 'charismatic' billionaire businessman Allen Stanford, saying: 'I'm proud to be associated with the Stanford brand and delighted they have asked me to serve as one of their global ambassadors. What they do is appealing and I've invested with them.'

This was just before it became apparent that Stanford had managed to lose $7.2 billion of investors' cash, with Stanford himself facing accusations of running the largest Ponzi scheme in history. We can presume that, on hearing this news, Michael Owen no longer believed 'what they do is appealing'. (Although he does appear to like losing lots of money.)

Since 2006, Michael Owen has also been global ambassador for Sport City, the sports theme park in the global capitalism theme park of Dubai. Since then, of course, Dubai has hit the skids, with expats fleeing the country and abandoning cars in the airport car park with maxed-out credit cards and ignition keys left inside. (I know, it's surprising Dubai has come a cropper in this recession, but it turns out that the whole thing was built on sand.)

Owen has also been a 'longstanding supporter' of the Jaguar brand – you can see where this is going, can't you? Oh, and what's the name of the company that appeared across his chest every Saturday at Newcastle? Oh, what is it . . . come on, what company sponsors Newcastle? Oh yeah, it's Northern Rock. Oh shit. Of course, he then moved to Manchester United, sponsored by AIG. What's he trying to do? Collect the full set?

Yes, these associations could be mere coincidence. But there is another, and I think more likely, explanation: that Michael Owen is a mystic avatar, a special child, who was sent by higher forces, to warn us. Perhaps looking back through history, before any great act of hubris, there we shall find Michael Owen, global ambassador, saying: 'What they do is appealing.'

So that's Michael Owen: sort of like an oft-injured Horseman of the Apocalypse, probably betting on all the other Horsemen of the Apocalypse. 'I'll have thirty quid on Pestilence, la! At the end of the world, I'll still be there scoring goals for England.'

P

Peaches Teaches

This is the name of Peaches Geldof's agony aunt column in the *Evening Standard*'s excellent *ES* magazine. But what can she teach us *exactly*? She's only fucking twelve and she lives in a hotel.

The five-star Mayfair Hotel lets her live at a knockdown rate so they can be associated with 'brand Peaches'. But what are the brand values of 'brand Peaches' – apart from being twelve and living in a hotel? And, er, just being Peaches? But no one else can be Peaches. Because they're *not Peaches*!

That's pretty much what I have learned from Peaches Teaches. Although admittedly I haven't actually read it.

Robert Peston

Robert Peston has 'had a good recession'. So much so that you have to wonder whether he and Vince Cable didn't conspire together to bring it on.

Peston beat Cheryl Cole and Bruce Forsyth to the title of Television Performer of the Year 2008 for his funny-voiced talking about banks. Even Mick Jones of the Clash popped up on the *Today* programme bigging up Peston as a man 'giving the truth to the people' just like, er, the Clash. That's true. It's not true, it's bollocks. But he did say that.*

Peston's book, *Who Runs Britain?*, was a runaway best-seller, bought by people who wanted to advertise the fact that they were the sort of person who could, if they really concentrated for a few hours, really get to the bottom of all this. Later. Look, I bought a book about it.

Anyone who did get round to reading *Who Runs Britain?* soon discovered it was basically Peston's typed-up background notes from the last few years stitched together and was not even greatly concerned with the crisis, having largely been written before the crisis, but still, it's got Peston's face on the cover, so who's really complaining here? There is, though, an extensive hagiography of Philip Green bordering on the homoerotic. Which is a bit weird. Has Robert Peston's brain somehow been getting Philip Green muddled up with Kate Moss?

* By the way, in another BBC interview, Mick Jones once revealed how he hasn't got a prepaid Oyster card as it allows The Man to keep tab of your movements. It's not that he just takes cabs everywhere or anything . . .

Phony Jade Goody relics
Makes a mockery of everything Jade stood for.

Polar bear picture specials
From their love of polar bears, you can divine the *Mail*'s love of the environment.

'LOOK MUM! IT'S BEEN SNOWING . . .' says the head-line, and there – here they are! – is a double-page spread about the beautiful, beautiful baby polar bears coming out of hibernation. A newborn is frolicking in the snow, biting its mother's ears, very much as nature intended. 'It's a sight to warm even the coldest of hearts.'

'On wobbly young legs, they emerge blinking into the early spring sunlight, amazed at a world where everything is a new adventure . . .' It's a real love-in. And they *are* cute as all hell.

Dead, dead cute. And, of course, if the *Daily Mail* has its way, actually properly dead. Because obviously they will happily kill anyone who even thinks of trying to stop their right to fly/drive/kill the planet, particularly screaming nutjob Melanie Phillips who calls climate science a 'massive scam', a 'pack of lies' and 'bad science'. (For her, to be fair, that represents keeping an open mind.)

Still, they're so cute, they will probably still be cute when struggling to survive in the last vestiges of their natural habi-tat . . . Ah, look at that baby polar bear trying to hang on to that ice shelf! 'Look Mum, it's not been snowing! Again!'

So look out for more wondrous picture-spreads to glad-den the cold heart. Don't look out for many polar bears, though. Because they'll be fucked. Completely fucked and dead and gone as much as if Ms Phillips had raised a pickaxe above their frolicking newborn heads and dashed their fuck-ing brains into the ice. That fucked. Which is *very* fucked.*

* I'm not suggesting for a moment that *Daily Mail* columnist Ms Melanie Phillips would kill a polar bear by raising a pickaxe above its frolicking newborn head and dashing its fucking brains into the ice until it is fucked. She'd probably get someone else to do it. No – I mean, she wouldn't do that. I'm not suggesting IN ANY WAY that *Daily Mail* columnist Melanie Phillips would kill a polar bear with a pickaxe. I'm just implying it a bit, which is not the same thing.

Polish delis closing down

Soon we will have arrived at the point where you can walk down a British high street – a *British* high street – and not find even a single Polski Sklep. And then what will have become of us?

I blame Europe.

Premiership 2

Hasn't even got its own name.

Prince Charles: 'I knew I was right'

The worst thing about eco-apocalypse is the opportunity it gives Prince Charles to claim he was right all along. Okay, maybe it's not the *worst* thing. But it's up there. Speaking to the *Sunday Telegraph*, the heir to the throne said: 'If now people are beginning to realise perhaps, after all, I wasn't talking complete nonsense, then I am delighted.'

He'd probably be delighted if people decided he was also right about homoeopathy and putting too much salt and sugar in the Duchy Originals products. Maybe people will even realise he didn't kill Diana.

On receiving his new 'being right about something' status, Charles almost immediately started undermining the democratic process by intervening in architect Richard 'Lord Rogers' Rogers' plans to turn the Chelsea Barracks in Chelsea into 'contemporary flats'.

PRINCE CHARLES: It's a carbuncle.
RICHARD 'LORD ROGERS' ROGERS: No, it isn't.
PRINCE CHARLES: Yes, it is.
RICHARD 'LORD ROGERS' ROGERS: No, it isn't.
PRINCE CHARLES: Yes, it is.
RICHARD 'LORD ROGERS' ROGERS: No, it isn't.
PRINCE CHARLES: No, it isn't.
RICHARD 'LORD ROGERS' ROGERS: Yes, it is.
PRINCE CHARLES: Ha!
RICHARD 'LORD ROGERS' ROGERS: What? Ah, shit!
THE COUNCIL: Sorry, you definitely can't build it now.
PRINCE CHARLES: I knew I was right.

Private jets

Before the crash, if you didn't show up to meetings in the newest of private jets, you would not be taken seriously as someone who would not do stupid things with clients' money.

But now they are on the back foot. Eco-protesters are chaining themselves to private jets as 'human wheel clamps' (although I reckon they just wanted to go for a ride). And then there's the fuel prices. According to P. Diddy, who is now reverting to commercial flights: 'Gas prices are too motherfucking high.' (I think I saw that news story too.)

Even so, they are still incredibly popular with CEOs who just don't give a fuck. Which is, at it turns out, quite a lot of them. JP Morgan Chase, which received $25 billion in TARP (US government bailout) funds, pressed ahead with purchasing two new luxury jets – plus a state-of-the-art hangar (how do you even have a state-of-the-art hangar?). CEO Jamie Diamond said: 'When I hear the constant vilification of corporate America, I personally don't understand it.'

Bet he understands it a little bit. Yes? A little bit? No? Little bit? No?

Really, of course, no one should be allowed to continue using these extravagant vessels of doom. Except, perhaps, for Iron Maiden.

Their new private jet is called *Ed Force One*, after the band's undead-psycho-zombie-godhead mascot Eddie. And it's not even a private jet – it's a customised commercial plane, a Boeing 757 (757 is the number of this beast).

With singer/qualified commercial pilot Bruce Dickinson at the helm, *Ed Force One* represents a major advance on the old-school van: band, crew and gear, in the sky, with the lead vocalist taking them to destination Rock. In a plane emblazoned with the famous Iron Maiden logo along the side and, on its tail, a mummified Eddie chewing through some chains.

So now they can rock up anywhere, at any time, to rock. Bringing rock to the poor, benighted peoples of the world? Taking rock wherever rock is needed? That's got to be worthwhile. 'Fasten your seatbelts – next stop Rock.'

Would Plane Stupid dare take on *Ed Force One*? I mean, that would be worth watching the news for . . .

Pro-capitalist demos

Much gets written about anti-capitalist demonstrations – right-wing and centre commentators waxing on their alleged incoherence, etc. But as they are mostly organised under slogans like 'People before profit', really it's quite straightforward to see the point of them. You do have to ask what a *pro*-capitalist demonstration might look like, though.

Small, basically. Probably people would start dropping out when you added things like 'oligarchs', 'arms trade' and 'child labour' to the list of slogans. (In the same way that millions will demonstrate against war in Iraq but melt away when you slyly start trying to get them to endorse Islamic fundamentalism.)

Anyone who actually tried to organise a pro-capitalist demo would have to be pretty mad and idealistic, you'd think. Thankfully, two libertarian bloggers were kind enough to confirm this suspicion during the G20, organising a counter-demonstration to the main protest.

Organiser Rory Hodgson rallied supporters of free market economics at the Bank of England. He rallied himself and his mate. So at least they had enough people to hold the banner up – even if one of them calls himself Old Holborn, does an online blog calling for things like a 'Straight Pride' march and was wearing a *V for Vendetta* Guido Fawkes mask – a shit mask from a shit film. A shit film that is in favour of anarchism. You silly twat.

Hodgson claimed state regulation, rather than market forces, is to blame for the recession: 'It is in the most regu- lated sectors — the banking and housing sectors — that this crisis has occurred,' he said. He meant it, too.

Their banner bore the slogan 'Who is John Galt?', a reference to Ayn Rand's super-weird 1957 libertarian/

sadomasochistic novel *Atlas Shrugged*, a bible for neocons. So at least they were getting their point across clearly.

Still, Mr Holborn proved he wasn't a complete fruitloop when he said state control of the money supply equates to 'fascism'.

Banners referencing dead ideologues, mind-bending utopianism, outlandish garb? These pro-capitalists aren't going to get *anywhere*.

Professors of poetry at war

Rhymers. Dissing each other. It's a bit old hat really – but academe's finally catching up.

When Derek Walcott was in line for the Professor of Poetry chair at Oxford, his rival for the post, Ruth Padel, sent emails to the press drawing attention to accusations from one of his former students. The press immediately dug out old claims of sexual harassment made against Walcott and labelled him a 'hound dog', notorious for 'preying on his female students'. He was eventually forced to withdraw from the race, launching the shaky defence: 'It wasn't me, it was, er, John Betjeman.'

Padel was appointed Professor, only to have to resign after nine days. No one was the victor here. As ever, literature offered some valuable lessons. And the lesson appeared to be: don't smear people using your own email address. Something like that.

It was all going off, though. Haikus. Limericks. Stuff you normally only see on sale abroad. At about the same time, Carol Ann Duffy was named the new Poet Laureate –

and she once wrote a long poem celebrating knife crime. Well, it didn't celebrate knife crime, but it was about knife crime – so had to be withdrawn from the GCSE syllabus, in case children saw the word 'knife' in a book and got too excited. (Duffy reportedly missed out in 1999 because of Tony Blair's fears about Middle England's reaction to a lesbian/bi laureate. 'Gay poets? What the fuck?!?' he screamed.)

Of course, poetry is no stranger to war. 'The Charge of the Light Brigade?' A poem. The First World War? A series of poems. So infused with the need for war was poet Simon Armitage, he got himself posted to Afghanistan.

Quite a drastic thing to do for inspiration. Still, if it stops him writing newspaper columns about really wanting to have been in an indie band, playing indie, then best of luck to him. Maybe it's even a new military strategy?

BRITISH HIGH COMMAND, HELMAND PROVINCE: Come out and lay down your weapons. We are calling a truce and sending in the poet Simon Armitage – the one who really wanted to be in an indie band – to lead you in a poetry workshop.
THE TALIBAN: Can't you send John Hegley? We much prefer John Hegley.
MULLAH OMAR: No! Ian McMillan! The Yorkshire poet! The Supreme Council have ruled that McMillan is the chosen one. Death to Hegley!

Then the Taliban charge and Armitage is driven away at speed in an open-top Land Rover, kicking up desert sand and making a screen between the fleeing poet and the futility of poetry. Silently, a tear makes its way down his cheek. He turns his face to the desert, so the soldiers cannot see him.

Property Snakes and Ladders

I did sometimes watch *Property Ladder*. I have literally no idea why this used to happen, but it did. It's still on, of course, only now it's called *Property Snakes and Ladders*. It's kind of a sequel, much darker in tone, revealing what happened to the people encouraged to become property players by *Property Ladder*.

In the first in the retooled series, Sarah Beeny met Natasha, a twenty-one-year-old woman from Leatherhead, who was utterly convinced that a couple of million was waiting just round the corner; from buying up properties and painting the walls white. So she spent her mother's equity on doing up a small house as the first step. Why did she want to go into property development?

'I have to say, my biggest inspiration was you,' she told Sarah. 'I've been watching you since I was about fourteen . . .'

Beeny shuddered: 'That's a bit scary.' Which it is.

When the market crashed and the profits dematerialised, Natasha was instead forced to move into the house with her mother (who had sold her other house). Even now, she wasn't giving up on those property millions: 'I will get there, but with a couple of years' delay.' (This time next year, Rodders . . .)

Many are now blaming programmes like *Property Ladder* for encouraging swaths of the population to see the nation's meagre housing stock as a source of ready riches, with inevitable results. '*Property Ladder*? Properly Fucked, more like.' That is what these people say.

Not that Sarah Beeny's having any of that. She's not to blame. She *always* warned that markets go down as well as up. Okay, so they never did go down. And she did write that book called *Profit from Property*. But it's not like the title was *Profit from Property – It's Basically Easy Money We're Talking about Here (Fish in a Barrel Doesn't Even Come Close to Describing What a Piece of Piss This Is)*. It was not. It didn't even have a subtitle. Subtext, yes – but not actual words.

Clearly, it's ridiculous to blame Sarah Beeny for absolutely everything that's gone wrong. There's also Kirstie and Phil. You can live here! You can also live there! Or over there! You can live bloody everywhere! Knock down a wall! That's Kirstie and Phil.

There's been some post-crash retooling here too, of course. On one particularly spicy edition of *Newsnight*, Kirsty Wark accused the other Kirstie (it was a Kirsty/ie-off) of selling a false prospectus that we could have it all and was now, with her homemade-cottage schtick, backtracking wildly.

Kirstie retorted: 'I happen coincidentally to be working on a different programme at the moment. Which talks about something I've always done, which is that second hand is best . . . that's what I've been talking about.'

It was second *home* stuff. Now it's second *hand* stuff. It sounds really similar, if you say it quickly enough. Aren't houses mainly second hand anyway? Of course they are!

Seriously, though, do you feel betrayed by Kirstie and Phil? Does *Phil* feel betrayed by Kirstie and Phil? Because by the looks of things, he also got swept up in the bubble (you know, *his bubble*) only to get caught out in the gooey aftermath: his property search company Garrington Home Finders was forced to shut up shop after a year.

So that's the second most famous property searcher in the land, gifted with hours and hours of free publicity on national television – the Property Search Guy! It's almost enough to make you think it was always just a steaming pile of horseshit – explosive horseshit. And you know what happens when horseshit explodes.

Still, I'll probably end up watching the odd one or two. You know how it is.

Pub closures

Pubs are closing at a rate of six every three minutes. Or was it six every three minutes? Anyway, it's a lot of pubs. Closing. Six every three minutes or something.

Since time immemorial, Britain's drinking culture has been based on the pub. It is the fulcrum around which all else revolves. But thanks to those supermarket lager deals, now our drinking culture has fanned out to everywhere else too. Even middle-class people have been targeted for getting shitted on wine at home all the time. What does this mean? Dinga-ling-a-ling! Last orders at the bar please, but for ever! No more orders! No more bar!

Okay, so it's mainly the shit ones at the moment. But watch out: soon it will be the fairly average ones. And after *that*, well . . .

Because when they came for the shit pubs, you thought, Well, I don't really like drinking in shit pubs, so er . . .

Q

Quantitative easing

The term was clearly chosen for its innocuous, impenetrable meaninglessness.

Say 'We're going to print shitloads of money' and people go: 'Fucking hell – Zimbabwe! Wheelbarrows! Rise of the Nazis!' (They always say those exact things, and in that order.)

But say 'quantitative easing' and they just shrug and go: 'That's a lot of "T"s. Ha ha!'

And, in a way, they're right. It is a lot of 'T's.

They didn't actually *print* the money, of course; they just made more virtual money by pushing a button that pumped it round the banking system. And that's supposed to put our minds at rest, is it? Magic money? 'Everything's okay – I've changed one of the numbers in the machine.'

'Thank fuck for that, for a moment there I thought you were just making this shit up as you went along.'

'No, not at all. Everything's under control. This new debt can just be bought off the Treasury by the Bank of England. They can probably find someone else to sell it on to at some point. Don't worry, you're dealing with the world's leading financial alchemists here. What can possibly go wrong?'

So it'll probably be fine. Maybe just bury some tinned food in the woods to be on the safe side, though, eh?

Queen as a style icon, The

Vogue started it, having the Queen photographed by Annie Leibovitz. The results were fairly tame by Leibovitz's standards, but the unused pictures of the Queen in the buff up a beech tree really are quite something, apparently.

Then with the launch issue of the magazine *Love*, style guru Katie Grand got Agyness Deyn to dress up as the Queen – hair dyed grey, blue satin, white gloves and tiara . . . Nice!

Turns out 'the face of the age' Deyn has collected Queen memorabilia – plates, flags – since she was a kid. Here she is talking about the Queen at a Dolce & Gabbana show: 'The Queen is my style icon. I kind of like the Queen mixed with, like, Ian Dury . . . d'you know, like, male female, old English, like flat caps, like scarves on their head, little twinsets, maybe like the punk queen.

'I used to look at pictures of her in her early days, with like all the jewellery . . . And like her hats and stuff . . . I love it!'

None of this makes any sense whatsoever, clearly – but she even collects Pistols-era Jamie Reid graphics of the Queen. This is definitely taking what you want from the punk ethos: in this case, pictures of the Queen.

In the *Love* pictures, Deyn could have *been* the Queen. Except they gave her a pouty, red-lipsticked kisser, *à la* Marilyn Monroe. People are, it seems, starting to get the Queen mixed up with Marilyn Monroe. And not just *Love* magazine.

'Spookily,' wrote Linda Grant, 'Monroe, had she lived, would have been the same age as the Queen.' Spooky! Not very spooky. But spooky! 'Even their figures – the large bust and small waist – are similar.' That's right, Linda Grant, and the Queen was pretty good in *Some Like It Hot* too, wasn't she? People have definitely underestimated the Queen's gift for comedy there, haven't they? Which one's bum was like 'jello on springs' again?

Okay, as of now, out there, on the streets, people are not dressing up like the Queen. The Kids are not pulling their hair back in a wavy thing and donning twinsets. Not, at least, to the best of my knowledge. I'm almost sure of it. I mean, are you dressing up like the Queen? Well, are you? (I bet you are, you mucky fucker. But that's just you.)

R

Recipease

The concept with Jamie Oliver's new delicatessens is that you can cook stuff in the shop, with friendly staff helping you and pre-prepped ingredients so you don't have to stand around in the shop cooking for too long. So it's like a readymeal, but more expensive, and you have to cook it in the shop. Come on, everyone, let's go cooking in a shop.

It's fucked up, fat tongue, and you know it.

Recycling rage

People are angry. It's rubbish, rubbish is. Rubbish is rubbish. Throwing it away is pissing people off. Recycling it is pissing them off. 'Residents angry over recycling.' 'Anger over bins axe.' 'Recycling centre sparks anger.' It's all that kind of caper. All over.

There is such anger, I'm surprised people haven't given in to their impulses and started attacking their recycling. Suddenly blowing their nut and really getting stuck in, passers-by trying to pull them off while they flail at plastic boxes of tins and things. Get some of this – you cardboard shit-fucks! And those milk cartons – they need a right kicking. Eat shit, A4-envelope with a plastic window cunt.

What I'm saying is: people are angry. The *Mail*'s Stephen Glover is angry. He's one of the angry ones, the refuseniks, the rubbish people: 'I would suggest,' he wrote, 'there is one issue about which nearly all of us care very much indeed, and yet it is hardly mentioned in high political discourse . . . I am speaking of rubbish collection, which, under this Government, has turned us into harried, persecuted and frightened citizens.'

(Bloody hell!)

'Rats and stinking bins are only the half of it. [The half of it!] There is also the problem of putting the correct things in the correct boxes.'

Ah, the boxes, the coloured boxes. Always the coloured boxes. Those bastard, bastard boxes. And the fines – oh, the fines! Glover hasn't actually had one. Neither has anyone he knows. But he's read about them. Oh yes, he's read about them all right.

'The threat of arbitrary fines [this is still Stephen Glover, by the way – he's still going, on the bins] . . . [makes] us feel like hunted criminals in our own homes . . . I feel the intrusion of state power *most closely* in my life every time my hand containing a yogurt carton hovers indecisively over a green or a blue box.'

It is, Glover concludes, 'a tyranny'. Do you hear? He feels like a hunted criminal. A hunted criminal in a police state tyranny. No wonder he's hiding out in his bloody loft! His family ferrying the poor bugger food! He only communicates by tiny taps! We're all bastards for letting this happen.

Thank God the *Mail* are on the case: GREAT WHEELIE BIN REVOLT . . . JOIN THE REBELLION . . . NOT IN MY

FRONT YARD! 'Householders are rising up in rebellion against the scourge of the wheelie bin.'

But then – well, it is only the bins. People are dying, ice caps are melting, cuts are on the way, a cent change in the cost of rice can leave millions of people literally starving . . . and you only get your bins emptied once a fortnight. Boo fucking hoo. It doesn't fit in the big bin? Then you're making absolutely *shitloads* of rubbish.

What is it with you, a hobby? HOW MUCH FUCKING RUBBISH DO YOU WANT EXACTLY?

Red Riding

Here are excerpts from an actor-stuffed three-part television spectacular I have written inspired by the experience of watching actor-stuffed prestige psychodrama *Red Riding*, the one with all the actors in it.

PART I: Anticipation

INT. LIVING ROOM. NIGHT. OTHER IS ON THE SOFA. SELF SITS DOWN. SELF CONSIDERS NEWSPAPER TV PAGES PREVIEW.

> Self: Bloody hell, there's some actors in this. Morrissey, Peake, Considine, Bean . . .
> Other: Bean . . .
> Self: And him out of *The Full Monty*.
> Other: Oh, and Warren Clarke. Do not forget Warren Clarke.

Self: I haven't.

Other: Want some tea?

Self: No. I'm too psyched.

FADE TO A BIT LATER.

Other: What's he done that for? What's he trying to find out? Who's that other journalist? What is that tie he's wearing? Who is that man?

Self: Er, he's gone to see Bean. To, er . . . It'll all become clear. Anyway, check out the 70s. Doesn't that just *feel* like the 70s? You know, polo necks, child murder, fags . . .

Other: I enjoyed the 70s.

FADE TO A BIT LATER.

Other: What's he done that for? Why did he do that with the car? He's bloody killed himself is what he's done. Is Bean dead? Was Bean there? How is Bean involved? I need to know if Bean's involved.

Self: Um . . . It'll become clear later.

CUT TO LATER.

Self: Um . . . It'll become clear in the next episode.

PART II: Confusion-Illusion

Other: Fucking hell, Paddy Considine's house is on fire.

Self: Yeah.

Other: So?

Self: Mmm. Just look at the acting, will you?

CUT TO LATER.

Other: Well? You wanted to watch it. Can you actually explain this to me yet?

Self: Um . . . It'll become clear in the next episode.

PART III: Just Confusion

Other: When is this? Is it a flashback? Fucking hell, even the present's in the past, this is doing my fucking bonce right in.

Self: Hmm. What mark Cortina is that?

Other: What?

Self: If it's a Mark IV I think we're back in the 80s again, so the 70s flashback is over. My uncle had one. It was white. The Mark II – that's the 70s, but the Mark IV is definitely . . . Actually it might have been the 70s. Oh, fucking hell. How much hair has David Morrissey got?

Other: Eh?

Self: How hairy is Morrissey?

Other: Only a bit.

Self: Right. So it's not a flashback. The hairier he is, the earlier it is. So this child murder scene is now – I mean, the 80s . . .

Other: What's all this swan's wings? Did Bean do it or not? Come on, man! The fat lawyer's gone through a trapdoor. But is the door real? Who is the wolf? What is the carpet? Who shot who in that club, and why? Where did Maxine Peake go?

Self: They had to chop it down from four episodes to three, so that's why it's harder to follow than the books – which are hard to follow anyway.

Other: We should try watching it without having had a drink. Are you taping it?

Self: I've had two small glasses of wine! I could legally drive a car – I should be able to follow a Channel 4 drama. It's Channel 4, for fuck's sake – the channel that brought us *The Girl with a Cock Where Her Head Should Be* and *The Friday Night Project*.

Other: *Friday Night Project*? I'd happily sew a set of swan's wings on to that pair of cunts.

Self: Indeed.

Matt Ridley

Matt Ridley is best known as the author of popular science books and also right-wing columns that pretend Darwin would have loved the free market. Darwin would have hated financial regulation too. That kind of thing. Whereas he should be far better known – far, far better known, by far – as a useless twat.

Ridley is an intellectual champion of the libertarian, minimal-state right – a former *Telegraph* columnist and *Economist* writer, and chair of a campaign that argues that only the market can safeguard the environment (a *slight* turnaround from his global warming sceptic past). The state should stay well back at all times: elephants should be hunted for their ivory and companies should decide if their food is safe to sell. Best before dates are the enemy of evolution. Whoever started putting best before dates on elephants is a cretin.

And, for a while, he did practise what he preached: he is singularly unafraid to get his hands dirty. Get his hands dirty picking up wads of filthy lucre for cocking everything to high buggery, that is. For Matt Ridley, ideologue of the free-market right, Mr The Cream Will Always Rise, Captain Sink or Swim was . . . wait for it . . . it's worth waiting for this, believe me . . . in charge of Northern Rock!

Oh yes. Matt Ridley, ideologue of the free-market right – the Honourable Matt Ridley, son and heir of Viscount Ridley of Blagdon Hall, Northumberland, that Matt Ridley – was non-executive Chairman of Northern Rock from 2004 to 2007. Up to and including that institution's spectacular implosion, when he was forced out of his £315,000-a-year post having, as I think we've already established, fecked everything up a right one.

Here he is in the *Newcastle Journal* in June 2007: 'In terms of raising money, we're very interested in a lot of overseas markets . . . the US, Canada, Australia, continental Europe and the Far East . . . We've got a huge market in the UK, we only have about 7 per cent of the market so far, there's no reason we can't get a lot more before we're done.'

Sadly, that didn't happen. Three months later, rather than picking up more than 7 per cent of the market, they sort of fucked the market completely. Perhaps it was all part of the plan: maybe in an 'If we can't have more than 7 per cent of the market, no one can!' sort of a way. Who knows?

Whatever was going on here, the subsequent wave of panic created the first run on a UK bank for almost 150 years and almost brought down the entire banking system (you may remember that; it was all over the news). Ridley once wrote that 'living beings are eddies in the stream of entropy'. And he was certainly a living being eddying in a stream of entropy at that point.

So what did Mr Market do? Let the divine hand of the market decide? Go down in a blaze of glory shouting to panicking Northern Rock depositors and employees: 'Fuck you! And fuck your state!'?

No. He rang the state and asked the state for help: 'Help us, the state! Please, somebody help us!' Or something very similar.

Darwinians evidently come in all shapes and sizes. Sadly, Ridley was widely identified as the 'weakest link' on the Northern Rock board. When the crisis unfolded (and Ridley was, in the subsequent words of the Treasury Select Committee, still 'clinging to office'), the *Guardian* noted: 'Step one ought to have been to order Northern Rock to find itself a proper chairman over the weekend. The current incumbent, Matt Ridley, is a science writer whose chief qualification seems to be the fact that his grandfather once held the post.' (Ouch! Still, it proves Darwin's maxim: It's Not What You Know, It's Who You Know.)

All Ridley was managing to do by 'clinging on' was 'damaging the good name of British banking'. Well, that was the Treasury Select Committee's view anyway.

Worryingly, as evolution often weeds out those who are not 'fittest' – most fit for purpose – Matt Ridley could well become extinct. Unless we act soon, this Matt Ridley may well be the last Matt Ridley we ever see on this Earth. An evolutionary dead-end. Like a dodo that's lost its mojo. Can we not get him on some kind of register?

Useless twat. Oh, I said that already.

Use–

less.

Twaaaaaaaa-t.

Okay, that's saying the same thing again, only in a slightly different way. I'll admit it.

Rogue biscuits

Not content with the eighteenth-century, £5-million-refurbed hospitality palace in Edinburgh, the fresh fruit flown in from Paris daily (sorry – but which fruit exactly is native to Paris?), and the acres of luxury carpet that had to be pulled up twice because 'Sir Fred didn't like the shade of amber', the execs at RBS took their biscuits seriously.

The three hundred dedicated hospitality staff were sent an email – subject header: 'Rogue biscuits' – that railed against the wholly unacceptable inclusion of pink wafers in the afternoon tea selection. The email warned that 'incorrect biscuit selection was a disciplinary offence'.

Cynics might say they could have spent less time worrying about whether there would be enough Malted Milks to go round and more time doing banking.

Ah, but they had that covered. On several occasions in 2006 and 2007 Sir Fred told the bank's board and the City that RBS 'didn't do' risky sub-prime mortgages. Very sensible of them.

Incidentally, the Royal Bank of Scotland owns – wait for it – one thousand pubs.

That's one thousand pubs. Not one pub, which could conceivably be an accident, or 922, which would be a more believable number, but 1000 (they even own Guy Ritchie's Punch Bowl in London). Like someone had suddenly yelled: 'Get me a hundred pubs, now – no wait, a thousand!'

And no wonder they pissed it all up the wall: they were pissing it up the wall. It's a wonder somebody didn't stop them when you look at it like that. Maybe that's why Fred Goodwin's always being driven around in all the pictures. Why in all his pictures, he is on the phone in a car being driven by someone else. Of course he's not driving. He's just left an RBS pub. And who's he on the phone to?

'I was at work . . . no, I am *not* slurring my words . . . I fucking love you.'

Rubbish presents as symbols of US–British diplomacy

Do they like us? I'm not sure they do. They send out such mixed messages. Do you think I'm being too needy? Did I sound like an idiot on the phone just then?

New relationships are always confusing at the best of times; those times being at the start of the relationship, always a time of confusion. That's why people read so much into the gifts exchanged between the Browns and the Obamas on their first star-crossed meeting.

Brown gave Obama a pen holder carved from the timbers of the sister ship of the Victorian anti-slave vessel HMS *Gannet* – which was deemed decent and correct. And in return, Obama gave Brown a box set of twenty-five classic American DVDs, in *Mail*-speak, 'a gift about as exciting as a pair of socks'. Presumably the *Mail* thinks giving away DVDs is their business. Maybe they think Barack Obama's copying them. He might be.

Sarah Brown bought the Obama girls some Topshop dresses and jewellery. In return, Michelle gave the Brown children models of the presidential helicopter, *Marine One*. In *The Times*, Sarah Vine slammed this shocking rudeness: 'It's not as though anyone needs reminding that Barack Obama is President or that he has his own helicopter. Short of giving the boys Action Man models of her own husband smiting the evil forces of neo-conservatism, Mrs Obama's gesture could not have been more solipsistic or more inherently dismissive of Mrs Brown.'

Okay, she could have tripped her up into some mud or something like that, but would that really have been as bad? Would it?

At the G20, the Browns gave all the world leaders a goody bag containing a tie designed by one of three British tailors (Ozwald Boateng, Timothy Everest or Richard James), a linen tea towel, a seventy-quid Kelly Hoppen candle, and some fancy chocolates.

A seventy-quid candle? How can a candle even cost seventy quid? It's fucking wax and a piece of string. You can do shapes and stuff, but you're still looking at wax and string to set fire to.

Showing a more personal touch, the Obamas gave the Queen an iPod containing photos of her last state visit to America. This showed the US leader's 'thoughtfulness', said the *Sun*, 'as the Queen is known to be a fan of iPods and has one that can hold 100,000 songs'.

What's thoughtful about that? He knew she already had one. Since when has it been thoughtful to get someone a gift you know they've already got? In return, the Queen and Prince Philip gave the Obamas a signed photo of themselves in a silver frame. Obama said: 'Yeah. Cheers.'

There's a world of nuance and powerplay to pick up on here, more even than at the summit itself. It's a tense business, with dangers lurking at every corner.

Imagine if the pen holder Brown gave Obama turned out to have come from a British slave ship by mistake. That would have been kind of funny, if very, very bad: 'I said *anti*-slave ship! *Anti*-slave ship! Oh, you bastards!'

Ryanair proposing to charge people for using the toilet on their planes

Providing people trapped several miles up in the air in your whizzy metal thing a place to widdle apparently constitutes a 'discretionary service'. Because clearly the expulsion of excess liquid and waste products from the human body has always been something of a pointless, luxury add-on to the whole life process, and the sooner people cease with all this toilet nonsense, the better for us all.

This new proposal was unexpected, even given the salami-style pricing policy of budget airlines. They keep headline fares down, while actually managing to rake in much more with their charges for not checking in online, a charge for a brown bag, a charge for a black one . . . four quid if you look at the check-in clerk a bit funny. Another three quid 'just for a laugh'. Plus the charge for weighing your hair.

Then there's the Hobbesian scramble at the boarding gate, as people batter old ladies and trample children underfoot for the absolutely vital opportunity to sit in one seat very much like all the other seats. It's an unseemly display somewhat reminiscent of dockers being made to fight for a day's work at the dock gate.

Now, though, there's Priority Boarding, or Speedy Boarding in jovial, orange Easyjet speak. By paying a tenner, you ascend into an elite, advance, smaller group of people battering old ladies and trampling children underfoot, etc.

Some people also seize the opportunity to stand around talking loudly about how they've got Speedy Boarding; like they've been made the fucking Mayor or something, the fucking freaks. Let's hope they don't get so excited they need a wee.

Ryanair boss Michael O'Leary has quite a distinctive approach to customer service, of course, once responding to a customer who'd sent in a complaint with the friendly missive: 'Look, you're not getting a refund so just fuck off.' Irish people can get away with saying shit like that.

Still, we're only one step away from this:

'The cost of your flight to Pisa is £22, sir . . .'

'Great.'

'. . . plus a tenner for the bag, and another one for checking in. Do you think you might need a piddle? A shit is a fiver. Then there's the onboard scratchcard game. Oh, and it's three pounds for us not to slap your face – I mean right across your fucking face – on the way through the boarding gate.'

'What?'

'Nothing, I didn't say anything. Also, we'll need to weigh your hair.'

S

Nicolas Sarkozy

It is on one level amusing that so many European leaders are such outrageous national stereotypes: Merkel the humourless bureaucrat, Berlusconi the corrupt authoritarian, and Sarkozy the randy little Frenchman. But how long can the EU remain a particularly fun episode of *'Allo 'Allo*? Because Sarkozy, at least, is in a profound state of flux that is leaving him almost unrecognisable from the cheeky Gallic right-winger of old.

'Monsieur Thatcher', the man who declared his intention to slash back the 'gluttonous', lethargic French state with a bit of Anglo-Saxon pep, has latterly been attacking 'fat cats' and the 'dictatorship of the market'. And Anglo-Saxon pep. He also denounced globalisation 'with everyone seeking, by all possible means, to take the jobs and markets of others'.

'Have I become socialist?' he asked, provocatively. 'Perhaps.'

From *ultra-liberal* to ultra-left. From 'candidate for brutality' to 'let a hundred flowers bloom'. This is heady stuff. But why this momentous transformation? Carla Bruni? Yes. But also – well, culture.

During the election, Sarkozy made much of being a cultural halfwit – loudly declaiming his love of shit French rocker Johnny Hallyday and declaring himself a 'total fan' of Sylvester Stallone. He made a massive deal of hating (literally hating) the seventeenth-century novel *La Princesse de Clèves*, attacking the person who put a question about it in a civil service entrance exam as a 'sadist or imbecile'. He'd had to read it at school and it was bor-or-ing. He never got over that.

But . . . by summer 2009, he was often seen carrying Émile Zola and Céline novels, and quoting liberally from the oeuvre of Jean-Paul Sartre (for fuck's sake). He also revealed he'd been kicking back with Visconti and Godard DVDs, and had been hanging out with deranged neo-nihilist novelist Michel Houellebecq.

Coming on top of the obsessive flaunting of his relationship with Bruni (they've been all the way, apparently), these ostentatious shows of pretension prompt one stark question: is Nicolas Sarkozy, the President of France, actually a student?

Shagging all day and reading existentialist philosophy? New Wave cinema? Trying to sound a bit left wing? He's probably also experimenting with weed and wondering whether he might be 'a bit gay'. Who can say?

He has even been trying to sound a bit 'street' – using slang like *'ch'ais pas'* for *'je ne sais pas'* and *'ch'uis'* instead of *'je suis'*. Come on – he's a student! He's a fucking student!

When he visited Pope Benedict XVI to receive the title of Honorary Chanoine of the Basilica of St John Lateran, automatically conferred to all French presidents, he caused offence by turning up late and then text messaging throughout his audience with His Holiness.

Late? Sitting at the back? Thinking it's cool to be texting when the fucking Pope's speaking? Student!

So, he's a student – clearly – but he's *also* the sixth President of the Fifth Republic of France. It's sort of fucked up. Maybe if he'd done a bit more tuning in and dropping out when he was younger, he wouldn't have become such a right-wing tool in the first place? Now I can say only this: get a proper job!

School bonuses

Teachers have spoken out about a 'bonus culture' in schools, with academy and foundation school heads often trousering over £150,000 a year including bonuses. The Copland foundation school in Wembley, West London, paid out £1 million to senior managers in bonuses over a seven-year period, while several heads have been caught topping up their salaries by appointing relatives to cushy jobs.

It's fucked up, clearly. The one place you'd think any reasonable society would want to fence off from market madness would be schools, rather than encouraging them to make hostile takeovers of each other and outsource PE to the Far East.

What do 'senior school managers' do, anyway? 'All those in favour of getting a load of kids together and teaching them stuff out of books say "aye" . . .'

Secret beaches

Holidaying in Britain. It's the new thing! We're not broke or anything, we just *really* care about the environment.

Anyway, it represents something of a problem for the style writer. There are only so many exclusive cliff-top boutique hotels to write about. (Two, in fact. There are two.) So instead they're reduced to coming up with things like lists of 'secret beaches'. Which is just kind of desperate.

There aren't any 'secret beaches' in Britain. All Britain's half-decent beaches have now been found. Show me a 'secret beach in Britain' and I will show you a 'beach in Britain that is fairly well used by holiday-makers'.

What it might be, I grant you, is a beach that many people in London haven't heard of just yet. But that would make loads of things secret.

Sexing up the snooker

Playing frames with six reds instead of fifteen, getting some halfwit to scream, 'Let's get the boys on the baize!' before every session. Then there's all the jump-cut BBC documentary-bio sections featuring block rocking beats, and Hazel Irvine with new variations on her trademark flicky 'do. It's time for frame nineteen of thirty-six – can you *feel* the tension!?!

But snooker is not supposed to be exciting. It's snooker. That's the fucking point. Of snooker.

You'd think they'd realise that snooker was the ultimate TV sport for recessionary times. You don't need a purpose-built stadium. You could easily just borrow a table for the duration of the tournament. It goes on for a long time in one place.

And that's what people like about it. Put one camera in

one position doing one shot all day and people would still watch it. That's how they like it. It's meant to be slow. Not sexy. Slow. Not slow and sexy. Just slow.

This is a sport in which Peter Ebdon – a bald man whose trademark style is to play very, very slowly (that is, in relation to a game that is already, as I think we've established, slow) – can have quite a sizable following.

The 'World' Championship (a.k.a. the Britain and One Bloke from China Championship) is regularly won by an interchangeable selection of tubby blokes who all have their surnames drawn from an absurdly small pool: Higgins and Williams mainly. Innovation in the game is someone wearing a slightly different waistcoat. The decision to stop requiring players to wear a bow tie took YEARS. John Parrott is about as horny as these people want to get.

And when you have pro-celebrity snooker it's at Pontins in Prestatyn and the one and only celebrity is Des Barnes from *Corrie*, who left *Corrie* in 1998. And – don't you *understand*? – that's good!!! Because it is.

Pace? Fuck your pace. This is snooker. Don't sex up the snooker.

Sky+/Freeview recorder road of good intentions

That is, deleting another entire history/arts/current affairs series to make way for a two-part docu-drama about the Norman Conquest and a series about Byzantine art – whatever that is – which, let's face it, you won't watch either, and will in turn be expunged for some other noble but ultimately forlorn attempt to fashion yourself into some sort of insane godhead of random knowledge (just like you always dreamed of being).

You wouldn't even momentarily consider deleting all your episodes – the watched-several-times episodes – of *Total Wipeout*. It never gets so bad that it comes to that. 'Don't take my *Wipeout* away, it's all I've got.'

That's what you say.

Patti Smith being big in 2010

In autumn/winter 09/10 'Patti Smith will be a big influence'. That's according to a tip-off by 'trendsetter' Catriona MacNab in a June 2008 *Guardian Weekend* article.

MacNab, Head of Trends at fashion-trend forecasters WGSN, knew this from checking in with people hanging out at music festivals and cool art shows and 'furniture fairs' – and by, er, speaking to the people who own all the shops, print all the textiles, make all the clothes, do all the adverts, etc. That is, the sort of people who may well have an idea of what people will be buying a year hence, as they are the ones who make/sell all the stuff you can buy.

Anyway, just in case: fuck Patti Smith. Fuck Patti Smith, fuck leather jackets, fuck being skinny, fuck talking about being an artist and definitely fuck quoting Rimbaud. I am so bored of Patti Smith. Even more bored than that time I listened to the album she did after *Horses*. And that's bored.

Apparently, autumn/winter 10/11 will be all about Bernie Ecclestone. Honestly, get the glasses and the hair now – I am NOT wrong about this.

Somali pirate toys

Kids love pirates, but this is just tasteless cashing-in.

Spandau Ballet, Return of

Many people greeted the return of Spandau Ballet with genuine delight: kilt manufacturers, for example, and people with no ears. I was sad, however, much preferring to keep them entombed in my memories. That would have been better by far, for me.

Gives them something to do, I suppose. Not that I'm suggesting they haven't been very, very busy – with their various ventures in film, telly, Tory fund-raising, sofas . . . Tony Hadley even markets his own range of golf balls.

And which self-respecting person hasn't, at some point, longed to club Tony Hadley's balls?

Phil Spector trial needing a retrial, The

One trial should probably have been enough. Apparently, after surveying all the evidence and finally finding the defendant guilty of murder, the retrial jury ultimately found itself 'haunted' by Spector's words to his chauffeur after staggering drunk, gun in hand, from his house, following the sound of a gunshot: 'I think I killed somebody . . .'

I would imagine that they did haunt them. If I was one of those twelve men and women, good and true, I would definitely have found myself struggling to overcome those particular words. I'm feeling haunted by them right now. 'I think I killed somebody . . .' Yes, I think you killed somebody too, you mad, mad bastard.

Incidentally, this is not the worst thing about the Spector murder trial – the worst thing about it was the murder – but it is still pretty terrible that the job he was doing just before that tragic event, Phil Spector's last production job, his last production job ever in a career that set many high water marks of music production, was producing . . . Starsailor.

I'm not trying to say it was their fault. Although I am trying to imply a small amount of guilt by association.

State-owned banks not paying tax (to the state)

Mere months after being bailed out by the taxpayer because they'd run themselves into the ground by being incompetent fuckwits, 'our' banks were spiriting away money through 'aggressive' tax-avoidance schemes. An early day motion alleged that Lloyds TSB, RBS, HSBC and Barclays – the first two heavily indebted to the taxpayer – had 'between them 1207 incorporated offshoots in tax havens to enable them and their clients to avoid and evade taxes . . .'

That's 301.75 tax-evading/avoiding offshoots in tax havens each on average. Crikey, that's a lot of tax-evading/avoiding offshoots – offshoots dedicated to shooting our tax into the stratosphere, where no one can find it but them. Not us. Them. It's something of a them and us situation we're looking at here. Our money. Their account. That sort of thing.

Now, I'm no accountant – but excuse me, that's our tax you're using to avoid paying tax! Even I can see that! Terribly sorry and everything, but isn't this just *slightly* – you know – taking the fucking piss?

There's robbing Peter to pay Paul, but this is like robbing Peter, going back to Peter to ask for more, using that money to pay your accountants to scoot the first money away to an offshore tax haven while Peter's wondering what has happened to all the money, then if Peter finds out, saying, 'Well, Peter, fuck you, you gullible arsehole. What did you fucking think I was going to do with it? Anyway, Peter, you know that money you gave me? I need a bit more. Come on, Peter, don't be such a fucking tightarse all your life.'

Don't know what Paul does. Coining it in I expect.

Sting's wife

Will people please stop referring to Sting's wife as 'Sting's wife'? She's a person in her own right for fuck's sake.

So don't say, 'Sting's wife took a private helicopter on an eighty-mile journey for an environmental gathering at Zac Goldsmith's house.'

Say, 'Sting's wife took a private helicopter on an eighty-mile journey for an environmental gathering at Zac Goldsmith's house.'

Supermarket land grabs

For the supermarkets, the recession changed the game. Asda was doing well. Waitrose wasn't but rallied with its new 'We Do Cheap Stuff Too' range. Lidl was a rising star, but was soon eclipsed by Sainsbury's. This was quite a thing to see; the public was warned not to look directly at Lidl during this time. Tesco wasn't used to all this and promptly announced a move into banking – well, the banking sector does need a trusted name that's not afraid to stick up for the little guy.

Most freakily of all, Morrison's was positively soaring. How did that happen? One minute it's all about Morrison's ballsing up the move 'down south'/buyout of Safeway and how it's all dowdy and cheap, and old Sir Ken Morrison's getting it in the neck from all quarters. Then there's a recession and, like a stopped clock, Morrison's is telling the right time. Why now? What's going on there? Why are good old-fashioned supermarkets with good old-fashioned colour schemes bordering on the grim suddenly back, back, back? Were there suddenly loads and loads more reasons to shop at Morrison's? Were there fuck.

All the supermarkets, however, were doing peachily compared to virtually every other retail outlet in the country. This opened up an opportunity – which they then duly took – for buying up those few bits of Britain they didn't already own. Anything remotely distressed was theirs: empty shops, retail park vacancies . . . all mopped up to become more supermarkets. (Tesco were even apparently using intermediaries to scoop up boarded-up pubs to pass on to them after planning permission is granted . . . Every little boarded-up pub helps.)

So in the boom-times, the supermarkets were grabbing all the land. In the bust-times, the supermarkets are grabbing all the land. What's happening here is that the supermarkets are grabbing all the land all the time. This part of the game hasn't changed – except that maybe it's got a bit faster. And cheaper for the supermarkets.

How many supermarkets can there actually be, though? Did you think there were a lot of supermarkets? I thought there were a lot of supermarkets. Turns out there aren't nearly enough supermarkets. There must still be vast swaths of the population going without supermarkets. Either that or something really fucked up is going on.

In the time it has taken me to write this, they have built a Tesco Express around me. So watch out.

Swine flu raps

No sooner had swine flu hit the news than various artistes had hit the studio to be the first to memorialise the pandemic with some sick beats.

The Streets' 'He's Behind You, He's Got Swine Flu' came complete with zombie-themed video of movie clips, only falling down on the fact that it is very difficult to contract swine flu, an airborne infection, from someone who is behind you. (The people behind *them*, on the other hand . . .)

Perhaps Mike Skinner should have read his government leaflet properly – and stepped in with some proper public service education: 'Dry your nose, mate . . .'

MIA seized the opportunity to update her 2007 single 'Bird Flu'; calling it 'Swine Flu'. So proving once again that she is one of the foremost chroniclers of the globalised age. Tackling all the major flu pandemics, yeah? No borders!

The best swine flu song is Lily Allen's forthcoming 'I'm Too Good for Swine Flu (I Don't A(H1N1) U)'. Internet leaks suggest it sounds exactly like all her other songs and goes: 'I'd thought we'd always/be together, But he said I had swine flu/And I never'.

Other verses go on to say that she never liked him anyway and his cock looks like a small badger's cock.

T

Teabagging protests

On National Tax Day in April 2009 various Republicans, Fox Newsy types and right-wing groups took up CNBC analyst Rick Santelli's call for people to get on the streets against tax – specifically, tax money used for bank bailouts and mortgage relief. They were inspired by the Boston Tea Party of 1773, when cargoes of tea were thrown into the water rather than unloaded as a protest against British taxes.

Things being what they are these days, the protesters decided to substitute teabags for loose leaf tea, and rather than just throw the teabags away – which would have been both symbolically and literally meaningless – to use the teabags to brew up insurrectionary but also thirst-quenching cups of, er, tea.

These rabid right-wingers – who want to respond to the collapse of hard right economics with, er, harder right economics – called these protests teabagging. Yes, they called the protests teabagging. Seemingly blissfully unaware that the word teabagging is the commonly agreed term for the practice of a man putting his testicles into another person's mouth. (Or, presumably, in his own mouth, if he's particularly athletic.)

Organiser Eric Odom called the protests a 'new day for the freedom movement'. Well it certainly sounds like it.

Come the anointed day, lots of US right-wingers were saying to each other: 'I'm into teabagging', and 'Would you like to do teabagging with me?' – confirming what we already suspected: that uptight right-wing homophobes often really just want to put another man's balls in their mouth. Maybe they could represent a tax double-whammy. Or tax bombshells.

Either way, they should just feel free and get on with it. Come on, guys – just put some balls in your mouth if that's what you want. No one minds.

There's no tax on balls. Not yet.

Ten Years Younger replacing the presenter with someone only seven years younger

Sadly for televisual cruel mistress Nicky Hambleton-Jones, television proved a cruel mistress.

After five series spreading the good vibes/telling people they looked too old and urgently needed some plastic surgery to stop them being so vile, she was replaced by someone younger, the acclaimed classical pianist and model Myleene Klass. You can't help feeling she had that one coming.

Mind you, surely the producers were missing a trick here. The acclaimed classical pianist and model Myleene Klass is only seven years younger than televisual cruel mistress Nicky Hambleton-Thingy. Come on, people, the clue's in the title!

The old Channel 4 wouldn't have slipped up like that.

To think . . . Peter Bowles narrowly missed out on being Jackie Brown.

Carol Thatcher

People used to feel sorry for Carol Thatcher . . . her mum was Margaret Thatcher, for fuck's sake! She was a celebrity and we got her out of there. Great days. But then she started coming on strong with the message that racist toys can be fun.

After she called French tennis player Jo-Wilfried Tsonga 'a golliwog' in a BBC studio, even the frothing demi-fascists of the more rabid right-wing press struggled to rally round: 'Yes, what she said was wrong, but has it come to this? Do we really want to live in a world where . . . oh, forget it.'

Charles Moore of the *Telegraph* did try to front it out for her, saying the remark was actually the embodiment of 'good will': 'When she said Tsonga resembled a golly, she was making a friendly remark, rather as someone of the same generation might say "Ooh, he looks just like Rupert the Bear or Noggin the Nog".' Yeah, because being told you look like Rupert the Bear is going to go down well, isn't it? With friends like that, eh?

It's the voters I feel sorry for. She's let down the *I'm a Celeb* . . . phone voters. Will no one think of the phone voters? Do their votes not count now?

Still, Ms T was unbowed. Appearing on the *Andrew Marr Show*, she revealed she loves the word: golliwog, golliwog, golliwog! That's her. But only because her generation think of golliwogs as harmless cuddly toys rather than madly out-dated black-slave grotesques. 'My store of golliwog fridge magnets has actually now gone up because people have sent them to me,' she said.

So that's good; her house is now a veritable haven of racist merchandise. I expect there's a golliwog on every available surface. She's probably got them hanging from the ceiling. (Not in a bad way, though.)

Thrift chic

It's the good housekeeping bandwagon. Saving money and weathering the storm aren't just boring necessities – they are cool. A penny saved is a penny gained. And many a mickle makes a muckle. Or does a muckle make a mickle? Shit, can't remember now.

The new queen of thrift is India Knight. When it was all about spending money in shops, India Knight wrote *The Shops*, about how great shopping is. Now it's all about not going down the shops and she's there too with *The Thrift Book: Live Well and Spend Less*. Shopping? So the year before last!

Inside, the insights come thick and fast. 'I wear Gap jeans, or ancient Levi's, and am very happy with them . . . If you haven't hung out in libraries since you were at school, give 'em a whirl . . . Scrabble – You know: you make words and score points and stretch your little brain . . .'

I was almost surprised she didn't just start explaining the rules: ' . . . there are double-letter scores. And triple letter scores. And double-word scores. And triple-word scores. And if you use all your letters, you get fifty . . .'

All in all, I'm not sure how much the book could be

described as 'value'. But then she does refer to the very specific figure of £12 as being 'cheap as chips'. Fuck me, they must be some chips. (Or maybe it's just *a lot* of chips?)

Alexa Chung's 'recession chic', again, clued me up on how to be poor but cool. In a series of poses in the *Guardian* modelled on Second World War propaganda posters (nice!) she extolled the virtues of locally grown clothes – like an £895 Mulberry jacket and a £1014 Stella McCartney jumpsuit. COME INTO THE SHOPS, said the posters: WE CAN DO IT.

'Yeah!' I shouted, punching the air. 'We fucking can!' It was the first time in months I'd believed that anything like that was possible.

They *were* nice clothes and everything but, you know, I'm not sure that India Knight or Alexa Chung are even that hard up. So when the style pages say, 'There's more than one way to weather hard times', you can't escape the feeling that you're being told how to weather the storm by people who think Storm is a model agency.

'Yahtzee! Do you remember Yahtzee . . .?'

Tiny particles

Even in an age of worry, with ready panic one of the few commodities to hold its own in all weathers, most people felt able to ignore dire warnings from scientists in autumn 2008 regarding 'wonder ingredient' nano-particles, widely used in thousands of everyday products, that might – might – act like asbestos on human tissue, or neutralise the bacteria that clean up the water supply. Aaargh!

It was heady stuff. The Royal Commission on Environmental Pollution called for 'major and urgent' action because these minuscule, little-understood, easily absorbed particles, a million times smaller than a grain of sand, and used in sun creams, car tyres, sports clothes and even medicines, are now in the water supply, being absorbed by animals, generally getting about ... even though no one knows very much about them, such as if they're safe.

The populace at large, already bingeing on bank collapse paranoia and surely ripe for a bit of pestilence, just shrugged.

Basically, scientists, it's the name: tiny particles. Be afraid! Be very afraid! 'But how can I be frightened of them – you've just said they're tiny.

'Now, *massive* particles, those I would be afraid of. If they were, like, the size of my head. Millions of particles the size of my head raining down on me from space. Aaaaargh! Now *that's* scary. But *tiny* particles? You're having a laugh. If they come near me, I will chin them.'

Now, swine flu – a name that conjures up images of fevered, sweating pigs – that's the sort of thing you start to panic about. Get a couple of Mexicans coughing and it's game on.

Tony Blair Associates
Will Tony Blair *ever* go away?

Just like the United States of America, Tony Blair has expansive offices in Grosvenor Square, London. Each of his notional initiatives/interests – climate change, Africa, money, etc. – has its own floor. So it's like a department store, only a department store that mirrors the inside of Tony Blair's head. The top floor is rumoured to be called simply 'Haberdashery'.

Tony Blair Associates is the name of Tony Blair's consultancy firm. World leaders can give him a call and he'll advise them on world leading, for a fee. So far, his clients are Rwanda and Kuwait, but I expect Saudi Arabia and China will be on the blower any day now . . .

Mainly, of course, Blair is getting back to where he belongs: the Middle East. As the so-called 'Special envoy to the quartet of world powers' – a parting gift from George W. Bush (to say sorry for all the nightmares?) – Blair's remit is to hang around in Jericho (like Jesus) and chat with Middle Eastern leaders; see if he can't move things forward in unspecified ways. Sort of like the dog whisperer – only with Israel/Palestine.

In practice, this involves turning up in Gaza three weeks after he could have done anything to help, surveying the rubble and announcing that it's 'terrible'. Like he'd only just noticed. Had he not been watching the telly? The massive furore. The world outcry. The daily pictures of suffering innocents. 'Oh, I was busy finalising my letterhead . . .' To be fair, it never stipulated that he would be 'special' in a good way.

With the Tony Blair Africa Governance Initiative, African leaders advise the man responsible for cash for honours and the false prospectus for war on getting his house in order. No wait, it actually works the opposite way round: Blair advises them on how not to get their house in order. Yes, that makes sense.

Moves to set up a Tony Blair Institute of International Relations at the London School of Economics were, sadly, quashed by academics. 'It would have been like the Saddam Hussein Institute for Human Rights,' one joked, only not joking.

But there is a Blair sports charity – the Tony Blair Sports Foundation – and he has set up his own faith foundation, whose modest aim is 'to bring all the faiths together'. It is called the Tony Blair Faith Foundation. He really should have stuck with the first idea: the Tony Blair/God Foundation.

Oh, and he's manoeuvring feverishly to become the first President of Europe. Or, if you will, the Tony Blair Europe Foundation.

You might imagine one flaw of Tony Blair Associates would be, well, who would want to associate with that scary failure? And you would be wrong. Blair is currently the world's most highly paid public speaker, outstripping even Ronnie Corbett, charging £400,000 (or £6000 a minute) for two lectures in the Philippines, which contained such nuggets of deep wisdom as: 'Politics really matters, but a lot of what goes on is not great.' And also: 'Religion [can be] a source of inspiration, or an excuse for evil.' At least Corbett's got some good golf anecdotes.

Plus Blair trousers £2 million a year as an adviser to the investment bank JP Morgan Chase – there's real synergy here, they like being involved in unholy shitstorms too (Enron, Madoff, WorldCom, etc.). And there's another £500,000 from Zurich Financial Services, where he mans the phones at lunchtime.

Don't knock it, though. There is a lot of experience here.

And he's finally done some thinking. Indeed, it's worth savouring Blair's final summation of the economic boom that underpinned his term in office – that sainted time of peace and prosperity. (Well, not peace, obviously . . . or real prosperity . . .)

In December 2008, at a question and answer session with students at Yale University, he said: 'I have, unfortunately, come to the conclusion that it was luck.'

Will he ever go away? No, he will not *ever* go away.

Tory artists

Tracey Emin was the first artist off the blocks to express an interest in supporting the Tories. Of course she was.

She told the *FT* that she 'voted for Boris' in London's last mayoral election (in an interview in which she 'groaned' about Gordon Brown's income tax rise). That's Tracey Emin, the self-professed Thatcher-hater. But that was then and this is now. 'I now realise that she was not really a Conservative but a Thatcherite,' she says.

So there we have it, Tracey Emin has it on good authority that Margaret Thatcher was not a Conservative (not really). And the Conservative Party has utterly repudiated what it now considers its darkest moment: the Thatcher years. Don't remind them of those days for they will shrink and cringe from the memory of Thatcher. God no, not that again. Do not bring up the horrors of the past. Haven't we put all that behind us?

I thought an artist's job was to see through stuff. Not to see through *less stuff than everyone else.*

She also announced that her 'favourite prime minister of all time is Ted Heath, health and education were his priorities. He wrote poetry, sailed, wore pink shirts and wasn't ashamed.'

That's old Ted all right. Not ashamed of anything. Although a proto-Thatcherite in his politics albeit he didn't like Thatcher personally. Brilliant.

The Conservatives are also reportedly 'targeting' Sam Taylor-Wood. Of course they are.

Tory C-words

Apparently, in Tory 'thinking' circles, cuts have been referred to as the c-word.

Sorry, chaps, you just can't say that. There's already a well-used, well-established Tory c-word, so that vacancy is sadly taken.

Tory Euro pals

The Tories have been very carefully trying not to look like freaks. But in Europe they've withdrawn from the Sarko/Merkel centre-right grouping, and set up a new one with proper looney-tunes parties instead. Parties like the Polish PiS (Law and Justice) Party (they heard about a Polish PiS Party and just had to get involved).

That's despite their status as Poland's premier gay-haters – that's the Polish PiS Party, not the Tories. One councillor from the party even attacked Poznan Zoo for adopting a gay elephant. Before you know it, there'll be pink elephants everywhere.

But it's not all hating homosexual elephants. The Tories' planned new coalition is actually very varied: there's also the Czech Civic Party which was founded by someone who thinks global warming is a myth. 'Actually, I think you'll find he's left that party,' William Hague countered. (So they're one of those freaky-founder-leaving-in-a-huff kind of parties. I like those parties too.)

And the Danish xenophobes who stood up to accusations that they were 'fanatical anti-Muslims' by saying, 'We are, in many ways, anti-Muslim' – they just weren't fanatical about it. And the Austrian Holocaust deniers led by the wife-beating weatherman.*

So, in essence, it's hard to say that the Tories aren't still mad about Europe. Sort of in a way that makes you wonder if they're still mad about everything else too – but are just slightly better at hiding it. Still, you do have to marvel at their willingness to embrace a side of Europe others would choose to ignore.

Imagine going Inter-railing with them: 'All right then, fancy going out to the patisserie for some really strong coffee?'

'No thanks, we're going to find a really bad bar full of homophobes. Catch you later, yeah?'

* Okay, I made that one up. But only that one.

Tory Jam fans

(To the tune of 'Eton Rifles' . . .) 'Tory Jam fans, Tory Jam fans!'

In those heady days of youthful discontent, the early 70s/late 80s, many Jam fans felt that the band's songs spoke about them, and in some senses for them – a generation condemned to dead-end lives on the margins of acceptable society: sink estates, ropy jobs, nowhere towns, all that.

In a way, the numerous avowed Tory Jam fans also grew up on the margins of society too. Different margins. As David Cameron explained: 'Going Underground', 'Eton Rifles' – inevitably, I was one – in the corps – it meant a lot, some of those early Jam albums we used to listen to.'

There is a logic here: if you were in the Eton College cadet corps, then at least one Jam song is definitely speaking about you, if not strictly for you . . .

'I really feel like that song, it's about *me*. You know, being an Eton Rifle. It's like they know what I'm feeling. Going out there – taunting the jobless. And you know they're always going on about society? Well, I bloody well *am* society. Balls, regattas, races, every bloody weekend! And 'In The City'? Yes, the City is one option, if I'm lucky. Well, I say lucky . . .'

And it's not just The Leader. Fellow Cameroonian MP Ed Vaizey – another member of what the *Spectator* called the 'Jam Generation' – went even further down the anti-Tory 80s pop road, fanatically supporting the hard left indie-soul outfit the Redskins: 'Russia sparked the fires in 1917 . . . The first workers' revolution in history.' The young Thatcher-lover liked the passion, if not the message. Even though what they were being passionate about was hating people like him.

He even liked 'Stand Down Margaret' by the Beat, saying: 'I couldn't work out what they had against Princess Margaret.' (He really did say that.)

Why did he stop there? He could have stood outside supermarkets selling copies of *Militant* newspaper – because he liked the passion. Perhaps start going on demos to bring down the capitalist superstructure, while shouting, 'Maggie! Maggie! Maggie! Out! Out! Out!' because he really enjoyed how passionate people were about getting this 'Maggie' person 'out'. Who could they mean? Maggie Smith? Maggie Philbin? And what was she even *in*?

'Tory Jam fans! Tory Jam fans!'

Doof.

TV shows/books commissioned in the high days of money worship having to be frantically and surreally re-edited to reflect the crash

So that's changing '. . . and that's why the super rich are the saviours of the earth' to something like '. . . and that's why the super rich are the saviours of the earth. *Or are they*?'

This would be Robert Peston's book, certainly. But mainly, and most enjoyably, Niall Ferguson's *The Ascent of Money*.

The TV version of Ferguson's paean to cash featured some truly odd, clunkily inserted pieces to camera dotted about, all concerning the credit crunch and mostly contra-dicting the bit you'd just been watching.

The book, meanwhile, was originally full of statements like 'the only species that is now close to extinction in the developed world is the state-owned bank'. And well – that won't do, will it?

So he had to add: 'though the nationalisation of Northern Rock suggests the species is not quite dead'. Stuff like that.

It was sort of like a game of intellectual Kerplunk where they desperately try to move sticks from their arguments without losing their marbles.

Fans of Niall Ferguson will be glad to know he was able to keep in the bits about Glasgow loansharks providing a valuable service.

Twenty-four-hour drinking

Does not exist.

Twenty20 cricket bloke, That

To unlock the mysteries of the Allen Stanford scandal, it is worth turning to the French intellectual Roland Barthes's 1957 essay 'The World of Wrestling'. Wrestling, says Barthes, 'is above all meant to portray . . . justice'. Ah. But 'good wrestling' is also an 'orgy of evil'. So you can see why your gran's so into it.

In wrestling, he continues, one wrestler is always the 'good' wrestler and the other is always the 'bad' – as in morally reprehensible, not less proficient at wrestling, although that too. The ugly one saying rude things is the baddie (Barthes calls him 'the bastard'). Then there's the one in the white pants. The one in the white pants is the good wrestler and the one in white pants always wins. Only an idiot couldn't get the plot here.

The point I'm making here is this: it is absolutely astounding that the world of cricket could not spot which one Allen Stanford might be. He had a moustache and wore a blazer. How much more obvious could he be?

He's like a cartoon villain straight from a 1970s sitcom. He even got other men's wives to sit on his knee, for fuck's sake – laughing naughtily and wiping mock-sweat from his brow. Short of being played by Peter Bowles, he could not have further advertised his imminent arrest.

'Blah blah . . . looking lovely today . . . blah blah, drinks everyone . . . ?' And the next thing you know, even Rigsby's lent him some money.

Even so, the England Cricket Board allowed Stanford to use Lord's as a heliport and essentially to hire the England team for a quids-up cricket-fest of his own devising in Antigua (and another, aborted tournament at Lord's). It's almost surprising they didn't try to get him to hire the England team as waiters for his next yacht bash. ('They'd be great – they won't drop a thing.')

It's hard to see how surprised they could possibly have been when the investigators finally went in, the subsequent banking devastation spread out from Stanford's Antigua base across Latin America and the man himself was charged with operating a $7 billion Ponzi scheme, the largest in banking history – including moving depositors' money from Stanford Bank to other parts of his group and then spending it on yachts and jets. Come on, it must have been above board. Otherwise it wouldn't have been signed off by the accountants – or accountant: an elderly (since-deceased) gentleman working above a hairdresser's in Enfield (true).

In the 'spectacle of excess' that is wrestling, says Barthes, the audience will this good and evil struggle. Wrestlers go through the motions of what the audience want to see. The audience make it so.

What made Stanford's audience (the cricketing world) reverse the mythology? Apart from the cheques, that is. People are taken in by Peter Bowles because they think they're getting in with the establishment: but cricket *is* the establishment. 'Allen? Had up for swindling? I can't believe it! I mean, yes, there was the moustache – but it's not like he twirled the ends or anything . . .'

So, yeah, just the cheques.

By the way, Quentin Tarantino once went up to Peter Bowles in a restaurant and asked if he'd have lunch with him as he was 'a big fan'. Bowles declined, as he'd already ordered a sandwich and 'didn't want to upset the waiter'. He has regretted it ever since.

Twitter
You know a fad has reached a tipping point when Lily Allen and the Queen get involved. The Queen is all over Twitter. Her Majesty sent her inaugural tweet during a Commonwealth Day service at Westminster Abbey. It read: 'Big shout to the UK. Much respect to the colonies, yeah?' It went down well.

Gordon Brown tweets. Sarah Brown tweets – keeping everyone up to date when she's at, er, Glastonbury. 50 Cent employs a ghost writer to compose his tweets. Britney Spears has a *team* of Twitter writers, all honing gems like: 'Went to the movies with the dancers tonight. We saw *I Love You, Man*. Sooooo funny!' And: 'Gone bonzo on the old drugs again. HELP ME.'

You can even enjoy Twitpics of Demi Moore's arse in sensible knickers, thoughtfully posted by husband Ashton Kutcher, or a Twitpic of Stephen Fry stuck in a lift. This is what humanity has come to – being very interested in pictures of Stephen Fry stuck in a lift. He tweeted regular updates: 'Still stuck in a lift.' 'Still stuck in a lift.' 'STILL stuck in a lift.' And: 'I'm out of the lift now.'

That guy who slags off the Internet all the time – a.k.a. Andrew Keen, author of *The Cult of Amateur*, and a believer that Web 2.0 is 'worse than the Nazis' and also 'communist' – blamed things like blogging and YouTube for creating a moronic world where 'ignorance meets egotism meets bad taste meets mob rule' – which sounds really cool. He said Twitter is 'just the latest, purest manifestation of narcissism and stupidity.' But he has his own Twitter page, the numpty. He tweets things like: 'Decaf or caf? Decaf or caf? Decaf? Or caf?' and 'Daily bran keeps me regular'. He is a huge tit.

Clearly these things are genuinely important, though. Because there are even now plans to teach schoolkids how to tweet. Real plans, put forward by the government. This seems mental – not in a standards are slipping way, more in a BUT THEY ALREADY KNOW HOW TO DO IT way.

The founders of Twitter (California-based geeks, somewhat inevitably) liken it to 'a flock of birds choreographed in flight'. Not 'a flock of shit yabbered against the void'. Having said that, I don't go along with the people who say it's *all* trivial.

In Moldova, people came into the streets to demand a recount of the general election due to the so-called Twitter Revolution. All the Twitterers were out on the streets. Well, except the one who kept tweeting things like: 'At gym. Well buff guy on treadmill', and 'What was that programme called with Kris Marshall out of *My Family* only it was on ITV?'

One of the instigators of the protests, Natalia Morar, had to go into hiding. She twittered regular updates. 'Still in hiding,' they said, mostly.

Some people tweet the Twuth. Eddie Izzard wrote: 'You are significant. Everyone is.'

Hold on to that. Thanks Eddie: we love you, man.

U

UKIP

Nigel Farage: crazy name, crazy guy, crazy ties, crazy pints, crazy lapdancing clubs, crazy fags.

He and his United Kingdom Independence Party are combating 'faceless, unelected' Eurocrats by getting their weird faces elected. In the June 2009 elections, people were (reasonably) alarmed by the BNP's successes, but it was UKIP whose vote went skywards by capitalising on the disillusion felt towards both main parties following the expenses claim. This was weird, though, given that Nigel Farage had claimed £2 million in MEP's expenses. This was, he admitted, 'a vast sum', but he wasn't a stinking hypocrite because he wasn't lining his own pockets. He was merely lining his party's pockets. And all in a good cause.

So Farage: he's quite crazy. But is he crazy *enough* to lead UKIP? Maybe that's why he had to stand down. He said it was to concentrate on standing against Speaker John Bercow, but this is, after all, home to the 'humorously sexist' MEP Godfrey Bloom, who once said prostitutes like what they do and admitted he once visited a brothel (although he was too drunk to consummate relations). Then there was 'self-confessed' prostitute-user John Houston, the party's East

Kilbride candidate until he revealed his prostitute-loving ways.

Actually, at that point, he proved himself *too* crazy for UKIP and was expelled. Amazed at this turn of events, he grumbled: 'There's more to me – and they know this – than just someone who has used prostitutes.'

Just about crazy enough for UKIP, though, was the anonymous member who staged a hate campaign against the party's press officer Annabelle Fuller, subjecting the twenty-six-year-old to late-night phone threats, including a 3 a.m. missive calling her a 'whore'. Yes, the sex industry does appear to figure quite highly in UKIP-world.

I just don't know who I like best. Although I do know that the fact that voting for this bunch of utter, utter freaks is somehow being passed off as a rational protest against 'the crooks in Parliament' indicates one thing: that much of the UK has achieved partial independence from its fucking brains.

Incidentally, a book on the history of UKIP has been published. It's called *Hard Pounding*. So if you are interested in that kind of thing, that's probably your first port of call.

Don't put that title into the Internet, though. Not on its own, anyway.

Underground extensions

The London rich are hunkering down under the ground in metal-lined tanks. If that isn't proof they're up to something, I don't know what is.

In the twenty-seven months up to May 2009, Kensington

and Chelsea Council alone approved 616 underground extensions. Chelsea chief exec Peter Kenyon is building one under his Notting Hill townhouse garden. That's really showing dedication to your local turf – living in it.

The founder of London estate agents Foxtons, Jon Hunt, is building a five-storey mansion – under his existing Kensington mansion. Christ on a bike, what are you doing down there – bowling? Oh, you are. So you've got a bowling alley *and* you've got a cinema, you'll probably be wanting the multi-storey car park too. Oh, okay, you will be parking your collection of sports cars down there. Wonder if there's somewhere crap to eat pizza.

Saudi royals are going one better with a £50-million, fifty-room super-home in Belgravia. But that's just showing off, isn't it? The bedrooms will be upstairs (which is a bit square), with that all-important underground space reserved for the pool and servants' quarters. Lucky old servants.

By the way, it's not all plain, er, digging. When Swedish property tycoon Gerard Versteegh started gutting the frame of his West London house, he had to stop work in a panic as the house next door started to fall into the hole. The neighbours had to be evacuated, and immediately launched a legal action against him. Stop sniggering at the back.

University of Google

And you thought Google only wanted to control all data . . . the new operating system to displace Windows, the censoring themselves in the interests of the Chinese Communist

Party, the displaying of pictures of the entire world ...
Turns out that's only the start of their ambitions.

Google is setting up its own university, the Google
University. It will be next to the Googleplex, Google's underground bunker HQ – which is itself like a crazy university
campus (well, there are adults riding scooters, anyway). It's
also a major funder of the Singularity University, a new place
of learning – also backed by NASA – dedicated to exploring
all cutting-edge technology, but mainly the possibility of
living for ever.

The chancellor of this new university is author, scientist
and general madpants future-gazer Ray Kurzweil, who is, it's
fair to say, utterly obsessed with the prospect of no longer
having to grow old or die. Or, indeed, be human. Kurzweil's
ideas are controversial, amounting to what one sceptical rival
called a mix of fine food and 'the craziest sort of dog excrement'. (Normal dog excrement would be bad enough.)

His vision of 'singularity' is all about letting yourself be
taken over by nanotechnology, thus transcending old-
world biology and changing up to become man-machines
with brains that are 99 per cent nanobot. He's not mental or
anything.

So this is what happens when Net geeks become richer
than anyone could possibly imagine. They set up universi-
ties devoted to living for ever with a robot brain. Christ, what
does Google's action plan look like?

1. Supersede Microsoft.
2. Supersede humanity!
3. Get off with hot chicks.

V

David Van Day, prospective parliamentary candidate

Okay, everything is a mess – the economy, Parliament, everything else – but exactly who looks at that mess and says: 'What we need here is David Van Day'?

One person does that. And that person is David Van Day – one half of shit 80s pop duo Dollar, hotdog salesman, *I'm a Celebrity* . . . reject, latter-day Bucks Fizz revival member who nabbed the name Bucks Fizz because 'I built that name up.'

The one who former Dollar partner Thereza Bazar calls an 'awful, vain man' and who dumped his girlfriend live on Channel 5's *The Wright Stuff.*

Yes, *he's* the one to hose out the stench of corruption and clean the goddamn place right up.

In a sense, it's only logical that the Brighton-born Brighton resident should want to take on expenses star Nadine Dorries, Tory MP for Mid-Bedfordshire. Dorries was alleged to have claimed for a hotel room for New Year's Eve and a second-home allowance for her first home (presumably getting confused by the whole second-home concept). It was also reported she claimed for a lost £2190 deposit on a rented flat.

David Van Day hates that kind of shit.

Anticipating his visit to the constituency, he said in a press release: 'It will be great to see the town that boasts the famous Woburn Abbey and Safari Park.'

Now, I could be wrong here, but that sounds a bit like he'd just looked it up on the Internet. I'm surprised he didn't say: 'It will be great to see the town that boasts the famous Woburn Abbey and Safari Park (citation needed).'

Anyway, it's good to know we've got people of character coming out of the woodwork, along with Esther Rantzen, whose dedication to reining in her famed ego in the name of public service took a knock when she compared her role to that of Oliver Cromwell.

Even outdoor-romping *Apprentice* superstar, and self-professed 'queen of bitches' Katie Hopkins had a go at standing as an independent MEP (strangely not getting elected).

Why not, though, when Gordon Brown tried to entice GMTV's Fiona Phillips into his 'government of all the talents'? And, er, Lord Sir Alan 'Sir Alan Lord' Sugar off *The Apprentice*. That's back before he started taking his line from Joanna Lumley.

Maybe they've all cottoned on to an evident truth: that many people in Britain would be happy to live in a fascist state provided it was run by Jamie Oliver or someone their dad fancied.

Violent bankers

Definitely the worst sort of bankers.

In the States, top bankers are usually 'abrasive bull street-fighters': that's urban toughs who are also – somehow – bulls.

During the meltdown, Bear Stearns boss Jimmy Cayne let rip on new US Treasury Secretary Timothy Geithner. 'This guy thinks he's got a big dick. He's got nothing, except maybe a boyfriend.'

Cayne was angry. Seemingly because the US Treasury Secretary did not have a big enough dick (even though he thought he did) (which he didn't) (the arsehole).

Cayne continued: 'I want to open up on this fucker, that's all I can tell you.'

At RBS, Fred Goodwin's daily meetings were nicknamed 'morning beatings', with one executive claiming: 'You sense that he could tear you limb from limb, and you are ever so grateful when he doesn't.'

Well, it's just unnecessary, isn't it? Even if he didn't actually beat anyone – which he may have, of course, let's not rule it out.

Anyway, we knew about all the testosterone flying around, but it seems even the women were at it. At HBOS, Head of Risk Paul Moore's 'going too fast' warnings made him so unpopular that one female exec cracked: 'She stood up, she leant across the table and said, "I'm warning you, don't you make an effing enemy out of me."'

Bet she didn't say 'effing' either. This is one in the eye for those who imagine a City run by women would resemble some kind of hippy festival. Unless they mean Altamont.

Virtual recession

You thought things were looking dicey in the real world. Wait till you see Second Life. The value of the Linden dollar – the internal currency of the online escape-world – has plummeted. Turned out it was all a big bubble that had no real basis in reality.

W

Walls separating the rich from the poor

Good fences make good neighbours. But then, a fuck-off three-metre-high wall makes non-existent neighbours. And some people prefer that by far.

In the great cities of the world, the gulf between rich and poor is so huge that people often talk of metaphorical walls. But then one well-to-do district of Buenos Aires started constructing an actual massive great wall dividing itself from a poorer neighbouring district. Build walls, not bridges!

After public outcry, the government stepped in to stop construction of the high 'Wall of Discord', and reinstated the metaphorical barriers, which everyone found to be much more satisfactory.

To be fair, the neighbourhood had clubbed together to build this wall, so the communal spirit wasn't entirely missing.

Westfield shopping centre

Ten years in the planning, five in the building, costing £1.6 billion and conceived as Europe's biggest 'retail destination', Westfield was a West London shopping Babylon combining high-end shops like Gucci and Prada with other shops selling other clothes that looked similar but didn't cost as much. 'This has never happened in the UK before,' said Mary Queen of Shops (and she should know – about shops). Never – that's never – had there been so many shops. Not in one place, anyway.

Yes, there was the odd controversy along the way: mooted death of other shops, too much traffic . . . Local residents complained about the noise and dust from the building site, and also of rats being accidentally let loose. Rats! How the hell did that happen? 'Did you just let the rats loose?' 'It was an accident!'

It opened in October 2008 – almost to the day that the banking crisis hit and the recession blasted the maxed-out-mega-shop economy out of the water and the *New York Times* claimed 'the recession has aimed its death ray at the very ethos of conspicuous consumption'. Suddenly, this was 'a monument to another age' (said the *Guardian*).

You could *almost* feel sorry for them. Was this not, after all, a too-perfect symbol of the massive hubris that has afflicted us all? The Westfield Group – the Australian mega-mall-builders behind the project – probably noted as much at the very next meeting. 'What we're looking at here is a too-perfect symbol of hubris,' someone probably said.

Then someone else added: 'Maybe at the opening we shouldn't have shouted, "Look on my works, ye Mighty, and despair!" That seems a bit silly now.'

Still, I bet the ethos of conspicuous consumption isn't *that* dead – credit card companies are reportedly starting to rake in the profits again.

Maybe the death ray was just set to stun!

Wet-look leggings

They don't look wet. They just look shiny. So if you do want to look like you have just wet yourself, then they are NO USE whatsoever. Don't believe the hype!

Windows Vista

A vista is, of course, a view. Sadly, I cannot see anything at all, due to my computer being completely fucked.

The Wire, People going on about

It's the show everyone is talking about.

Still.

'I'll tell you what I've been watching. It's this programme called *The Wire*. Have you seen it?'

'Yes. I've seen *The Wire*.'

'What season are you on?'

'Season three.'

'Oh, okay. I'm on four. It's great.'

'I bet it is.'

'Still, season three is good.'

'Yes. It's amazing. Nothing else will ever touch me in the same way again.'

'Sure . . . four's better, though.'

'So how's it different, then?'

'Well, it's hard to explain . . . it just sort of goes off into a whole different place.'

'What: Philadelphia?'

'No, it's hard to explain. It's more like a whole other reality. You wouldn't really understand. But yes, sometimes Philadelphia too.'

'It's really opened my eyes to the whole urban American experience. It's made me think about things in a new way – and I've been really getting into hip-hop.'

'I know, me too. I'd always liked hip-hop, but I never knew there was so much good stuff from Baltimore.'

'It's the best hip-hop there is.'

'I'm going there on my holidays. Taking the kids down the West Side.'

'Good idea. We went last year. West Side *and* East Side. I think I prefer the East Side, actually.'

'Have you heard about the sixth series?'

'There's a *sixth* series?'

'It never got made. But there were plans. It was going to be set in the City Parks Department. With a whole thing going on between rival park attendants – everyone competing to keep the place free from litter and general antisocial behaviour. Then some people were going to get really fucked up and it was going to spin off from there . . .'

'Of course, I really love *The Shield* . . .'

Woolies

Greatly missed. Mostly – if not exclusively – by fans of Pyrex.

Working for no pay

Doing voluntary work can be a great, worthwhile and ful-filling thing. But not if it's just your normal job without getting paid. That's not a great thing. Not even a bit of a great thing. That is a shit sandwich.

British Airways chief Willie Walsh really put himself out there, agreeing to work unpaid for the whole of July 2009, forgoing his July 2009 salary of £61,000 to help 'save the company' (yes, he did earn another £61,000 the next month). He was really going without. And asking his employees to go without too.

'Fancy working for no money? You know, only if you want to. No pressure . . . You won't be, like, first in line for the sack if you refuse or anything. (You will – you fucking will.) What? No, I didn't say anything . . .'

Working until you die

Given the collapse of pensions and provision for the elderly in general, it is good to know there's another option. Who needs rest anyway? You're only as old as you feel. Although, it has to be said, one does tend to feel older, the older one actually is.

Turns out that working until you die isn't all bad, mind.

It does at least help to avoid dementia. On the down side, you do have to keep working until you die. Having dementia might have helped a bit there.

Still, you do get free prescriptions.

World cinema displays in high street music/DVD retailers that are basically just all the films with nudity and shagging in them

Visiting one prominent high street music and DVD retailer, the only one left in fact, they had an entire end-of-aisle, double-width display of world cinema DVDs – *all* of which featured covers promising some 'sex action'. Not just some of them like before.

Lower City (eh? Eh?), *Anatomy of Hell*, *Ages of Lulu* (I bet she does), *Sadomania*, *Belle de Jour* (I bet it is) . . . and, brilliantly, *Swedish Erotica*, all lined up exuding come-hither raunchiness. Thirty-two films in total – many with beautifully lit ladies reclining in their scanties on silken sheets, or even – even – pictures of women's actual breasts on the cover. And that's not *Swedish Erotica* the mucky vintage porno, you understand – that's *Swedish Erotica* the kitsch classic of Scandinavian cinematography. Of course it is.

Times must be tough in the world cinema market if retailers are basically reduced to saying: 'Look! There's shagging in these films! Tits! And arse! There's tits and arse! Tits! And arse!'

Let's hope that HMV doesn't start applying the same sex-it-up treatment to world music – particularly given the preponderance of elderly Cuban guys who have lost a lot of their teeth.

Wrong green jobs, The

When the Danish wind turbine company Vestas announced it was to close its Isle of Wight factory (the only wind turbine plant in all of Britain), Climate Change/Energy Secretary Ed Miliband (not the banana Miliband brother who talks like a textbook; the other one) was busy announcing the need for green jobs. What a fortunate coincidence. Miliband was all about creating green jobs making things like wind turbines. So you'd think he'd be in there guaranteeing these green jobs – the ones that already existed. He didn't even need to create them, but they'd still count. Result!

Er, no. Clearly, Miliband felt it would be far more sensible to lose the workforce's accumulated expertise, build a new plant from scratch somewhere else (or not even build one at all, you know?), and let the job losses impact on the already struggling Isle of Wight economy. Yes, that would seem like the most obvious course of action in the creation of 'green jobs'. To a fuckwit.

He explained his decision thus: 'If we expropriate the factory . . . some people might not like that within a capitalist system . . . and we also need lots of other wind turbine manufacturers to come and invest here and I don't think it would be encouraging to them.'

We can prop up banks, that was essential, but propping up wind turbine factories? Are you mad? That'll send the whole system into turmoil! It's not like they're doing anything useful – not like the banks. And where will it all end? If we start propping up *some* green jobs, then we'll have to start greening the *whole* economy and *then* where will we be? Did you think about that?

The wrong sort of green jobs, then – like the wrong sort of leaves. Except the wrong sort of leaves stop trains. So actually not like that.

Perhaps the wrong green jobs are more like Wallace and Gromit's wrong trousers, in ways that we just don't understand yet. Maybe, er, a criminal penguin that moved into his back bedroom made Miliband do it?

Come on . . . there must be some sort of rational explanation.

<u>X</u>

X-Factor for scientists

As we know, no area of human endeavour can fail to be enhanced by introducing a competitive, fame-contest element including a large prize, a panel of feisty judges and, preferably, a text vote. Not even physics.

Enter FameLab, a contest which the media dubbed '*X-Factor* for scientists'. A series of regional heats and video entries culminated in a final that smashed popular preconceptions about science students: second prize went to a talk about 'Green Fluorescent Monkeys', and third prize to one on 'Aliens'. There weren't many girls there.

But the winner was Tom Whyntie from Imperial College, London, who grabbed the £10,000 prize and a slot on Channel 4 for a presentation on the Large Hadron Collider (LHC) at CERN in Switzerland. CERN, you may remember – and I'll try not to be too technical here – is where they try to smash particles together in a big pipe in order either to a) find God or b) BLOW UP THE FUCKING WORLD.

Whyntie's talk hinged on how it would be 'a result' if the £5-billion experiment found nothing at all. This is true, as it would mean they hadn't BLOWN UP THE FUCKING WORLD.

They are also trying to find 'dark matter' – which may,

or may not, make up the unidentified fifth of the universe. Er, right, so now they've mislaid, like, a fifth of the universe? Someone needs to keep an eye on these fame-hungry maniacs. Particularly knowing what these contests can do to even the sturdiest of minds.

Best watch out, or we'll be grey goo before you can say 'phone lines are closed'.

Definitely don't bother voting after that. It'll be a *complete* waste of your time.

X-rated not being the same as porn

The first people to feel the full force of public ridicule in the expenses scandal were then-Home Secretary Jacqui Smith and her bearded husband, Jacqui Smith's husband. At least when the whole scandal broke in full, the weight was also borne by others. Then again, even after that, they were still the only ones found to have claimed for watching dirty movies.

But how dirty were the dirty movies? That was the question. When asked for clarification, the Home Office refused to disclose that information. Yes, Smith's spokesperson explained, the two movies in question were X-rated but, they added, 'X-rated is not the same as porn.'

True enough. But why wouldn't they disclose exactly how dirty these films were? We need to know these things. Was it national security? I thought we were supposed to live in a free society, with the free flow of information – we, the people, need to know exactly whether these films were among the X-rated films that are also porn or whether they were the X-rated films that are not porn, but simply too disturbing or complex for non-adult eyes. And it raises more questions than it answers: is X-rated *erotica* the same as X-rated porn? I just don't know. And *they* won't bloody tell you! What have they got to hide?!

By the way, a report in the *Daily Telegraph* reckoned the films in question had been broadcast on Television X and were called *By Special Request* and *Raw Meat 3*. So they probably were porn.

Y
<hr/>

Year of Hugh Laurie, The

The French have gone mad. Mad for Hugh Laurie. And that's fucking true.

House (or *Dr House*, as it's called in France) is a massive, massive hit, a 'phenomenon'. Laurie's long-forgotten spoof spy novel, *The Gun Seller*, is firmly installed in the best-seller lists (at one point being the bestselling title in all of France). Hugh Laurie has 'charm', they say; he has 'class'. He is 'irresistible' and also 'unstoppable'. (That's right: Hugh Laurie *cannot* be stopped. Even if they wanted to. Which they don't.)

Hugh Laurie is sexy. The celebrity magazine *Voici* called Laurie 'the greatest seducer in the world'.

Hugh Laurie doesn't play by the rules. 'He is so cynical and so politically incorrect. He's misanthropic . . . He has no time for following protocol,' gushes Valerie Hurier of *Telerama* magazine (possibly of House – but is not House Laurie, and Laurie House?).

Hugh Laurie is emotional. One magazine declaimed: 'With Hugh Laurie, you don't sleep, you laugh. With Hugh Laurie . . . you are moved . . . It's the year of Hugh Laurie or it's no one's year at all.' (Yes, they are talking about the Hugh Laurie who used to do the piano mugging. That

Hugh Laurie.) (You 'don't sleep', though? What the fuck does that mean? What: never?)

Now, Hugh Laurie seems affable enough, and best of luck to him, but I definitely think I'll make it through the year, indeed most years, without being touched *in my whole being* by Hugh Laurie.

In fact, I would say I will remain largely *un*-touched by Hugh Laurie.

I might watch a couple of *Jeeves and Wooster* re-runs on ITV 4 if it comes on after *The Professionals*. Even if this does move me, which it may, I still think, hope and believe that other things will have a greater hold on my consciousness across the span of the entire calendar year.

No disrespect to Mr Laurie himself, of course, because, as I say, he seems very affable and – actually, you know what, he is pretty good, isn't he? Sort of unconventionally handsome, if vulnerable, but in a clever way. He . . . hmmm . . .

Maybe I do want to be touched by Hugh Laurie. Caressed by him even, like I matter to him and am the *only* one in the world that matters to him, the damned mixed-up fool. He wouldn't even need to shave. In fact, I'd prefer it if he didn't. Love me Hugh Laurie, love me.

Y-fronts revival, The

Y-fronts are back in front. And at the back too. Sales are up and pants are on. Why? Because the flapping-free boom-times are over! FOR EVER! That's why.

At times like these, a man needs to have snug balls.

According to Debenhams – who should know about this shit – sales in Y-fronts have increased by 35 per cent since The Difficulties began.

Of course they have. Going to a sensible shop like Debenhams and buying some old man's pants and popping your gentleman into them: that's what makes a man feel safe in straitened times. Better that than to run the risk of being castrated by, er, not sure.

Warm and safe. That's the way.

YouTube spam

To be scrupulously fair, I do admire these people's workrate. To insert an advert for your hot MILF swingers site into the discussion thread under nearly every single video posted by the millions of YouTube users worldwide does represent a level of dedication and downright industriousness that we're always told is lacking these days.

It's still stupid and irritating, though. All you're trying to do is while away the seconds until death by watching obscure clips of The Faces who, let's face it, you don't even like that much but it does beat working . . .

don'tstopthenight (2 days ago):
The early 70s . . . Rod was true to his rock n roll roots back then, solo or with The Faces. Excellent!

bluemagoo (1 day ago):
Is this Rock 'n' Roll?????

xmo99er [1 day ago]:

Looks like Nicky Hopkins on piano? These guys rocked, what a great band.

captaincaptain [1 day ago]:

Nope . . . that's the great Ian McLagan . . .

cottoneyejoe [1 day ago]:

Definitively Faces it was a great band.
Awesome

zebb27849 [1 day ago]:

for hot teen babes, go to hotteenbabes.com. they're hot.

yeswe'realonenowtiffany2 [7 hours ago]:

Thats an Armstrong plexiglas guitar Woody is using. The proto-type was used by Keith during the Stones' 69 tour.

A variation on this is certain users' obsession with grading any female by how 'hot' she is. Any female at all. This is not limited to music clips featuring gyrating honeys, but extends to serious actresses involved in moments of high drama (say, Charlize Theron in *Monster* ('hot!')) and even footage of German Chancellor Angela Merkel . . .

hoochiecoochieman [7 days ago]

SOOOOOOOOO HOT.

jimbo12 [6 days ago]

She's, like, the hottest.

hoochiecoochieman (6 days ago)

Yeah, a hottie.

jimbo12 (6 days ago)

Hot stuff.

hoochiecoochieman (6 days ago)

A hot one. Hot – to – trot.

mangodave (4 days ago):

I don't like her.

yeswe'realonenowtiffany2 (2 days ago):

Thats a vintage Ralph Lauren blazer she's wearing, from the Spring-Summer 98 collection. The one with the three-button cuffs.

zebb27849 (2 days ago):

for hot teen babes, go to hotteenbabes.com. they're hot.

Mackdog98 (1 day ago):

The blouse is *slightly* stained on the collar.

Z

Zavvi

All the high-profile high street businesses that have gone tits up so far have begun with letters from the dark end of the alphabet: Woolies, Whittard's and Zavvi.

And is that just a coincidence? Er, yes it is.

In the case of Zavvi, though, it probably is relevant. It was called Zavvi, for fuck's sake. It's a rubbish, rubbish name. Why – why? – did they call it Zavvi? When the company bought out Virgin (which didn't go tits up despite starting with 'V', lending credence to the whole 'coincidence' theory), managing director Simon Douglas explained: 'Zavvi reflects a modern take on the word savvy; both knowledgeable and clued-up'.

But going round replacing 'S's with 'Z's – for no fucking reason – does not scream either knowledge or clue, or even the ability to spell.

It just sounds stupid. 'Juzt popping out for a zandwich, Zimon.' Zee?

Anyway, it doesn't matter now.

Z-list celebrities feeling the pinch

It's sort of comforting to know that celebrities are feeling the economic pain too. Maybe 'comforting' isn't the right word . . . okay, yes, it is the right word.

John Malkovich, Zsa Zsa Gabor: both scalped by Madoff. Kevin Bacon too. Hence the new parlour game: Seven Degrees of Bernie Madoff.

Carol Vorderman had to slash the asking price on her Thames riverside flat by £800,000. And after all she'd been through with *Countdown*.

Leonardo DiCaprio was the same, having to cut the price on one of his three LA beachfront properties. Not the *Countdown* bit.

Even *Cash in the Attic* presenter and money-saving expert Lorne Spicer had to file for bankruptcy. She tried selling off the contents of her attic – but it came to the usual, essentially useless sum of £215.12.

It has been a shock for us all. But now it is time to move forward. And we look to our celebrities to lead us. People like Tamara Ecclestone, daughter of Formula One billionaire Bernie, whose life has been literally turned inside out by the recession: 'I have definitely cut down on my shopping and stopped being so spontaneous . . . For example, I have a bikini from last year I can wear again, so I don't need to buy another.' She's doing her bit – why aren't you?

Mainly, of course, we must look to Tracey Emin. In particular, to the truths she speaks in her column in the *Independent*. At first, she played her cards close to her chest. Sly old, wise old Tracey. Mostly during the crisis her columns furnished us only with details on what time she'd been getting up in the morning, whether she'd been really pissed-up recently (or not so much) and, obviously, stuff about her fucking cat.

But I knew she would not fail us. And sure enough, in October 2008, she punctuated a column mainly concerned with the 'new girl' at the *Independent* to whom she dictates her column with this excoriating tirade against the status quo: 'I'm bored of what I'm being told. I'm so bored of nobody knowing what the right answers are. It's obvious what the answer is. We've been at war for twenty years – this country and America – what does anybody expect? Where do we expect all the money to have gone? Just gone down some stupid pit, some stupid hole.'

Taking all the money and throwing it in some shitty hole? Tracey Emin hates that crap. And so should you. No wonder everything's gone to fuck!

She is right to be concerned. Even the artists – yes, *even the artists* – are suffering in this climate. Prices of Damien Hirst pieces have collapsed. At one sale in New York, one of his dot paintings priced at £2 million failed to attract a single bid. Damien Hirst: do you even remember that arsehole?

But Tracey Emin's prices have actually risen. Tracey Emin is one of the very few people on Earth *not* to be feeling the pinch. 'I think I am pretty credit-crunch proof,' Emin said. 'I have sold more . . . than I ever have before.'

We've had credit bubbles, property bubbles, energy bubbles, commodity bubbles . . . And now, finally, proof – if more proof were needed – that humanity *still* has its head up its arse: the Tracey Emin Bubble.

Come on, Tracey, maybe you should think about popping your head outside the bubble sometimes. Rather than just still – STILL – crapping on and on and on and on about yourself.

Otherwise what you are doing is WASTING EVERYONE'S FUCKING TIME.

Acknowledgements

We would like to acknowledge, primarily and foremost – and fulsomely – our estimable publisher Antonia Hodgson and our illustrious agent Karolina Sutton. Scott Murray added some valuable ideas and text, for which we salute him. We would also like to thank Sean Garrehy, Hannah Boursnell, Kirsteen Astor, Diane Spivey, Andy Hine, Nathalie Morse, Andrew Edwards and everyone else at Little, Brown. And Laura Sampson and Tally Garner at Curtis Brown.

Also a big thanks to everyone whose talkings and writings helped us along the way, in particular Rick Blackman, Cath Fletcher, Damon Green, Dorian Lynskey, Terry Williams and John Higgs.